THE
PRIVATE
INVESTIGATOR'S
HANDBOOK

THE
PRIVATE
INVESTIGATOR'S
HANDBOOK

CHUCK CHAMBERS, P.I.

A PERIGEE BOOK

THE BERKLEY PUBLISHING GROUP
Published by the Penguin Group
Penguin Group (USA) Inc.
375 Hudson Street, New York, New York 10014, USA
Penguin Group (Canada), 90 Eglinton Avenue East, Suite 700, Toronto, Ontario M4P
2Y3, Canada (a division of Pearson Penguin Canada Inc.)
Penguin Books Ltd., 80 Strand, London WC2R 0RL, England
Penguin Group Ireland, 25 St. Stephen's Green, Dublin 2, Ireland (a division of Penguin
Books Ltd.)
Penguin Group (Australia), 250 Camberwell Road, Camberwell, Victoria 3124, Australia
(a division of Pearson Australia Group Pty. Ltd.)
Penguin Books India Pvt. Ltd., 11 Community Centre, Panchsheel Park, New Delhi—
110 017, India
Penguin Group (NZ), cnr. Airborne and Rosedale Roads, Albany, Auckland 1310, New
Zealand (a division of Pearson New Zealand Ltd.)
Penguin Books (South Africa) (Pty.) Ltd., 24 Sturdee Avenue, Rosebank, Johannesburg
2196, South Africa

Penguin Books Ltd. Registered Offices: 80 Strand, London WC2R 0RL, England

PRINTING HISTORY
Perigee trade paperback edition / September 2005

PERIGEE is a registered trademark of Penguin Group (USA) Inc.
The "P" design is a trademark belonging to Penguin Group (USA) Inc.

Library of Congress Cataloging-in-Publication Data

Chambers, Chuck.
    The private investigator's handbook / Chuck Chambers.
        p. cm.
    ISBN 978-0-399-53169-9
    1. Private investigators—United States. 2. Investigations. I. Title.

HV8093.C48 2005
363.28'9—dc22

2005048938

PRINTED IN THE UNITED STATES OF AMERICA

I would like to thank Susan Brown, for her long hours of work, as well as Joe Kane and Gentry Austin for their help with this book.

I appreciate my family enduring my long nights and my grumpy mornings.

Thank you all for helping me; without you it would not have been possible.

CONTENTS

INTRODUCTION

I DIDN'T INTENTIONALLY set out to become a private investigator; the job came to me. It was 1982, and I had made a career change, leaving the Palmetto police department after five years as a patrolman to open up a small window and door repair business. During my time with the Palmetto PD, my beat was the back alleys and packing houses, a rough neighborhood. I received three letters of commendation, one for stopping an armed robbery in progress. One of the advantages of working for a small-town police department was that you had to learn to do everything yourself. There wasn't a detective or crime specialist on call, like the CSI TV shows. We had to do it all ourselves. I took advantage of the opportunity by learning as much as I could, taking all of the special courses that were available to me.

In 1980, I was assigned to the county drug task force. I became very aggressive on the war on drugs, so much so that the local drug dealers got together and issued a contract on my life. At the time, I was living in a rather remote area with my wife and kids and I feared for their lives. We decided that the risk was too great for the relatively low pay and relocated for a time to Wyoming. After two years, I returned to Florida to open a small window and door repair business, hoping for a quiet, simple life. But one day, the phone rang and changed all that. It was "Howard," a former prosecuting attorney in Manatee County, Florida, with whom I had worked with on several cases during my years as a cop.

"The reason I'm calling is because you did a good job as a police-man, and I have a problem that I thought you might be able to help me with," he said. "I have a client whose ex-husband is coming in from Texas and has court-ordered visitation for the weekend. He has threat-ened my client with abducting the children and taking them back to Texas. I want to hire you to follow them the whole weekend to make sure he doesn't."

I took out a pad and paper and began to scribble notes.

I agreed to help Howard and his client. I called up my good friend Jimmy to ask if he wanted to help. We started tailing the mark after he arrived in town, following him as he picked up his children and drove about seventy-five miles to a small town up the Florida coast. The man swung into the driveway of a ranch-style home set back off a gravel road, surrounded by orange groves.

Just my luck. A quiet country setting with no other houses nearby and a lot of wide-open space. Not a very good place to set up a twenty-four-hour, undetected surveillance. The only thing I could do was seek cover in the middle of the orange grove that would still afford me a field of view of the house and driveway. We found a suitable spot right next to a pond about 1,000 meters from the house and settled in for a long, hot weekend. And it was long, because the husband never left the house with his kids. The next day was Saturday and by noon I could tell Jimmy had questions on his mind. He finally blurted them out: "When are we going to eat and what are we going to eat?"

We raked our cash together for a total of $5.65 and drove to the nearest country store. Walking in the front door, we passed a shelf loaded with chewing tobacco and advertisements for Pabst Blue Ribbon beer. It became increasingly clear as we strolled the aisles that five dollars was not going to buy us much food for the rest of the day and for Sunday.

I paused at the back and looked up at a small display of "Willie's Famous Fishing Kit." It was a plastic pack with a few hooks, a bobber, and about twenty-five feet of line. Jimmy and I smiled at the same time and knew Daniel Boone would have been proud of our thinking.

We bought the fishing kit and headed back to the orange grove and the pond. Jimmy strolled about, catching grasshoppers, while I rigged two fishing lines with hopes for dinner.

Well, in short order we caught a half dozen small perch and then it dawned on us: We had no way to cook them—no pans, no forks, no plates. We both shook our heads and wondered what the hell we were thinking as we sat on the ground, leaning back against the truck.

I felt something digging into my back from the pressure and, shifting around, glanced at the front tire just as Jimmy said, "Hey, we can pop that hubcap off and cook them in that."

Jimmy took the hubcap down to the pond to scrub off the road grime while I dug around in the truck for any liquid to cook the fish in. Way in the back, a dusty can caught my eye, and I raked out a can of Budweiser beer that must have been under the seat for months. We poured the beer in the hubcap, made a small fire, and cooked the fish.

By Sunday, the mark pulled out and dropped the children off at their mother's house. Our client was happy, and so was I—I had just made more money in one weekend than I normally did in a week.

I dismissed it as an adventure until about two weeks later, when the phone rang again, and it was another lawyer I didn't know, asking, "I got your name from Howard, and need some help." So began my new career as a full-time private investigator. Now, 20,000 cases and twenty-two years later, I have decided to pass on the tricks of the trade and the techniques that I've developed to those who want to become their own private investigator.

You may think you won't ever have a need for a private eye or for these skills and tools. But when I ask people why they want to hire me, many of them say it's for some "peace of mind." Not knowing the truth about business, family, spouses, a legal case, or an unknown adversary is a major reason why many clients call me. But when they hear my hourly rates, they often realize they can't afford one. I charge $75 an hour for infidelity cases, plus expenses. That can add up to a few thousand dollars during a typical weekend of surveillance. But the good news is that you can do most of the work if you learn the same techniques and acquire the same tools used by professional investigators. In the chapters that follow, I will give you real-life examples of cases I've handled in the past. In each case, I'll walk you through the steps I took to solve it, the very same steps you can take to solve your own case. The names of course, have been changed. Hopefully, this book will save you money, and perhaps your marriage or your business, and give you some peace of mind.

I do have some general advice before you take on your own case. The first is, be honest with yourself and examine your own motives— why are you doing this? Use the information in this book responsibly, legally, and for the right reasons. Let your conscience be your guide when it comes to lying or telling the truth. All I can do is tell you what the professionals do and point you in the right direction. You have to answer to yourself.

There are always as many sides as there are players in life's dramas. That's why I've provided a chapter with the flip side of each situation that might call for a PI. For every person trying to find hidden assets, there's a person with assets to hide. For every person shadowing a mark, there's someone trying to evade surveillance. I'll tell you how to find out everything you can about a person, and I'll also tell you how to protect your privacy so you can't be found. A private investigator is hired for all of these situations.

I also want to pass on a few cautions before you start playing detective. First, private detection is an art, not a science. Every case is different. Your case is one of a kind. The complications specific to each situation, the unpredictable behavior of the principals involved, the fickle weather, varying resources, your personality, and Lady Luck all form a unique stew that is your case. Your problem may only require bits and pieces from different chapters. Maybe your work doesn't involve electronic surveillance, yet you need parts of an intelligence report that will take you to the motor vehicle office to locate a license plate number. Maybe you don't need to find missing money, but you do need to tail someone. Much of detective work is not just taking action. It requires thinking on your feet and responding to the shifting landscape of the case. Yes, there are standard procedures, but prepare for the unexpected. Prepare to be creative. This is an art, not a science.

In addition, the laws governing the use of pretext (which is basically a phony script you use to obtain information) and electronic communications are changing every day. This also applies to computer information and spy programs. There are literally thousands of state, federal, and local laws and no one person can know them all or keep up with the changes. Before using the electronic surveillance tactics in this book, you may want to check the law or even consult a lawyer about their use. For example, in Chapter 7, under electronic surveillance, I will not discuss the use of audio techniques, such as planting bugs and secretly tape-recording, because it is illegal in just about every instance. However, you can set up hidden video cameras and conduct video surveillance, as long as the sound is turned off.

All of the techniques in this book have been employed for years by private eyes, but they are always subject to change. Many investigators have crossed the legal line and ended up charged in some cases. If you have a question, be safe and request legal advice on any topic in this book before conducting your own investigation. The information in this book offers an inside look into the world of private investigation, and is meant to assist you in solving your own case. The techniques offered in the following pages are within the grasp of the amateur, do-it-yourself sleuth. There are also more advanced techniques and equipment that I have not included, because these should only be used by professionals. However you choose to use this information is up to you; you do so at your own risk. I am assuming no responsibility for any tactic employed that fails to observe the law.

Next, I ask you to remember the old adage, "assume nothing." I've had many clients assume their spouse's lover was a coworker, when it turned out to be a best friend they've known for fifteen years. Furthermore, to work like a pro, you must try to remain emotionally detached. Emotions are your enemy when you're trying to gather evidence, especially in an infidelity case. Everyone involved in a case of this nature is prone to outbursts and irrational decisions fueled by emotions. Try to hold those feelings in check, or you'll blow your cover and your case.

To succeed at hiring yourself to do your own PI work, you also need to develop a solid plan before you begin. When I'm talking about a new case to one of my field agents here at the agency, the first thing that I do is have them make out an organized plan. In the first stage, they become familiar with the case—the addresses, cell phone numbers, vehicle descriptions, and any pertinent details regarding the circumstances of the case. As soon as this step is complete, we then develop an investigative plan, such as using surveillance, hidden video cameras, or doing records-retrieval work.

Finally, if there is any criminal or violent component to your case, call in law enforcement, a licensed PI, or your attorney immediately! Do not try to resolve these situations yourself. Although I have routinely worked on all of these types of cases, I have purposely not mentioned techniques related to domestic violence, child abuse, abduction, or violent crime. These cases are strictly for professionals.

In this litigious time, my goal is to empower the private citizens who need undercover legal assistance, but don't have the money to obtain justice or protect themselves, by hiring a professional. With this book, you can hire yourself.

ONE

HOW TO CATCH THE CHEATING BASTARD

WITHOUT A DOUBT, the majority of my cases concern infidelity. Many of the clients who hire me suspect their spouse is having an affair. And their suspicions are not without some foundation. Consider the following statistics:

- **Estimated percentage of spouses who have an affair in the United States: 65**

- **Percentage of my clients seeking this service: 85**

- **Percentage of my female clients whose suspicions are justified: 98**

- **Percentage of my male clients whose suspicions are justified: 50**

- **Percentage of divorce rate among the newly married: 65**

- National divorce rate: 40 percent

- Percentage of male parents who lose child custody requests: 92

- Percentage of female parents who lose child custody requests: 8

- Amount of alimony awarded annually in the United States: $87 billion

My clients may not be positive that their spouse is actually cheating, but they have noticed enough sudden changes in their behavior to know something is up. Their spouse might be working out at the gym more, or recently purchased new underwear, or are more attentive (or more distracted) than usual, or are volunteering their daily itinerary for no apparent reason. My clients might not actually have any hard evidence, like an unexplained hotel-room receipt or receipt for a romantic gift they never received, but they have noticed enough change in behavior to develop some strong suspicions.

Most of my fidelity cases begin with the sentence: "I just want to know; I need some peace of mind." And even if you live in a state that has a no-fault divorce law, you still might want proof before you break up your twelve-year marriage, stick a big alimony payment on your ex, and file for custody of your kids. If your investigation confirms a spouse is cheating, it is critical to gather hard evidence legally that can be used by your attorney in or out of court. In a no-fault divorce state, proof of adultery can provide key leverage in out-of-court negotiations. Often such evidence—for example, an unexplained pair of panties found under the backseat of your husband's car and preserved in a baggie—could be all the leverage your attorney needs to settle a case in your favor.

The majority of my cases are fidelity investigations in which my operatives and I collect such evidence. The cost can range from a few hundred dollars to break an unlisted phone number to $20,000 for long-term surveillance.

Unfortunately, many spouses cannot afford a private investigator. Many of my female clients have husbands who control their finances and only allow them a small allowance, so they are unable to hire a private investigator. This book is written for them.

Such was the case with a client of mine called "Rita." As do most controlling egomaniacs, Rita's husband, who was a prominent doctor, kept control of their funds. This particularly pissed off Rita, since she had forgone college herself and worked long hours as a waitress by night and a manicurist by day to put the tightwad through medical school. After he became Dr. Randall Smith, he gave her a modest allowance to maintain their household and raise their two little sons. Of course, the boys didn't know their father was cheap, because they really didn't know him. He often left before they woke up in the mornings and came home after they were asleep at night. And now he was spending even more time away from home. Rita suspected he was doing a nurse or a lab tech at the hospital.

Here are the steps that I took—that Rita herself could have taken—to determine if her spouse was unfaithful, to find out with whom, and to gather hard evidence that would nail the two-timer and make him pay. Big time.

CONFIRM THAT THE LOVER EXISTS

WE ALL KNOW there is something suspicious going on if we start receiving hang-up calls at the house. However, that's far from the only signal. Review the following list of signs to see if the person who said "I do" is in fact doing someone else. If nothing on this list applies to your spouse, then your husband or wife is either truly innocent, diabolically sneaky, or smart enough to have bought this book and read Chapter 2 before you did.

CHEATING CHECKLIST

IT'S TIME TO be suspicious when your spouse:

- Has a new interest in exercise and losing weight

- Buys you gifts without reason

- Tells you the boss wants him or her to work a lot of overtime on a "special" project

- Suddenly buys a pager

- Expresses little interest in sex

- Expresses more interest in sex

- Expresses interest in new sexual techniques

- Begins to dress differently

- Hides new fragrances or lingerie

- Begins taking longer and more business trips

- Has a new circle of friends

- Comes home smelling of alcohol or perfume

- Begins to leave for work early

- Shows little or atypical interest in family matters

- Makes several unexplained credit card purchases

- Begins to talk about wanting more "space" from you

- Is caught not wearing a wedding ring

- Has excessive and unexplained mileage on the car

- Spends an inordinate amount of time on the computer

- Comes home with suspicious stains on clothing

- Expresses a sudden and unexplained surge of energy

- Is always late

- Is overly protective of a briefcase, calendar, address book, organizer, and/or computer

- Expresses a new interest in eating different dishes

- Begins to buy new clothes

- Arrives home from work smelling of different soap and a fresh shower

Rita's husband scored an infuriating nine. He was definitely toast. There is no score that clearly indicates whether you should be suspicious, however. Frankly, any change in the normal routine and behavior could signal an affair. People don't change their routines and patterns for no reason, I'm afraid to say.

Conduct a Physical Search

Many suspicious spouses fail to conduct a thorough and creative search for the many types of evidence that might be relevant in a fidelity case. It may seem obvious, but you will want to begin with a methodical search of your spouse's car and private areas in the house. While it is true that you can have your husband's underwear tested for unfamiliar DNA (with a $24.95 semen-testing kit and $500 lab fee), a cursory and unscientific search for loose evidence is the place to start in your quest to confirm or deny that your other half is having an affair. As the spouse, you are in a better position than a PI to conduct this initial search for useful, incriminating evidence.

What to Look For

- Incriminating correspondence, such as letters, memos, notes, cards or e-mail (see below)

- Proof of gifts and secret purchases that you never received

- Receipts that you don't recognize

- Proof of trips with lovers

- Receipts from strange cities

- Plane tickets or boarding passes

- Motel receipts

- Credit card bills with these charges

- Visual proof, such as photos and videotapes

Where to Look

- Spouse's car (glove compartment, under the seats, and trunk)

- Bedroom (back of the closet, jacket pockets)

- Home office (briefcase, date book, organizer, address book)

- Garage (toolbox, storage boxes, leaf bag in the lawn mower—a favorite)

- Boat

- Shed

- Storage space

- Plane hangar

- Wastebaskets in the spouse's room, office, or bath

I gave Rita this list, then had her send the children off to school one morning and start at the back of Randall's closet. All she found was his ripped lacrosse stick from prep school and an unmatched tennis shoe. She had to move on to the office and garage before hitting pay dirt.

Rita found some unexplained appointments in Randall's date book and a greeting card with a sad-faced puppy on the cover in Randall's toolbox. The greeting said something like "Doggone lonely without you" and it was signed "Me," in a handwriting that wasn't Randall's, yet looked somewhat familiar. "Me?" Well, "me" wasn't Rita. She'd never buy a drugstore card with an idiotic, generic message. Who the hell was "me?" We were going to find out.

Hack Into Cell Phone Records

In any kind of illicit liaison, some type of communication—in addition to sexual—has to transpire so the lovers can get together. In today's world, that's usually done electronically—via cell phone, computer, and pager, just to name a few—and therefore leaves a trail. I like to start with the cell phone. If your spouse has a cell phone, that's the first place to look.

Assemble the Crucial Information

First you'll need to gather some information before you can hack into the cell phone records. You'll need the:

- Phone number

- Account number (which appears on the main page of the bill or on a cancelled check)

- Provider

- Official billing address

- Cheater's social security number

- Password—usually a mother's maiden name or favorite pet, hometown, or sport

During her twelve-year marriage to Randall, Rita had at least learned this much about her absentee doctor-husband: Randall had no favorite pet. He didn't like animals. Actually, he didn't like his mother, either. Rita had Randall's cell phone number and his cell phone account number from his cancelled checks, but did not have any records of his incoming or outgoing calls. Those records mysteriously never came home. Here are the steps you can take to access cell phone records.

The first step is to log onto the Internet and go to the provider's home page. Click on Access Your Account. Depending on what happens, you follow one of two routes.

If No Account Exists

Most cell phone users never access their accounts online, or even know they can do this, so they have not yet established an online account and thus a password.

Follow the prompts to the access screen and open an account. Enter the cell number. When the screen asks for a password, you instead click on Create a New Account and you'll be directed to a questionnaire. On this page you'll fill in:

- **Account number**

- **Name of the user (the billing name, which may be your spouse's Christian name or a corporate name)**

- **Typically, the final four digits of the social security number**

- **Either the mother's maiden name or the favorite pet name (This last entry will be a secret code word by which a client can access the system and recover the password should they forget it). Once you do this, the password will be forwarded to your e-mail (You may be required to log off the system and wait for your password to arrive by e-mail).**

Log back onto the system using your "spouse's" new password. Click on Access Detailed Billing. A complete list along with dates and times of all outgoing and incoming calls will appear on the screen. Print this out. (Eventually, your attorney will have fun waving these pages about the courtroom.) Scrutinize the records for repeated numbers that you don't recognize, especially those that occur during his travel to and from work and at lunchtime.

I discovered that Randall was calling the same number every morning as soon as he left the house. Could this explain his leaving two hours early for work every day? Incoming calls from that number also came in throughout the day to her husband's cell phone.

If There Is an Account

If your spouse does have an account, you will need to hack the carrier in person to secure the password. For this you will have to do what the professionals do and use a pretext—a script.

- Employ a male family member or friend (or female, if you're checking on your wife).

- Purchase a voice changer for $39.95.

- Call the carrier with the phone number and account number claiming to have forgotten the password.

- Be prepared with your spouse's social security number, mom's maiden name, and the name of their pet.

- Explain that you've changed your e-mail address and provide the new address—yours.

You Have the Number, Now Identify the Homewrecker

Now that you have the phone number, you're ready to identify the tramp or prick who's ruining your life. If the number is published, you can find the name and address using a reverse telephone directory. If your spouse's other significant other is using a cell phone or has an unpublished number, you will need to employ a pretext or script.

If the Number Is Published

Log on to the Internet and use a reverse telephone directory such as Google.com, 411.com or www.freeality.com-finde.htm. Put the area code and number on the search line and press Enter. If the number is listed, the name and address of the owner of the telephone will appear. If it is a cell phone or nonpublished number, the screen will report Not Found.

If the Name and Address Are Not Available

If the information is Not Found, which means the lover is using a cell phone or has a nonpublished number, you have two choices: Engage a private investigator like myself who has the means to break the number and secure a name and address, or hire yourself and employ a basic pretext. This means calling the number and getting the name out of the owner herself or himself by using a time-tested pretext or script:

- Block your identity either on your own phone by using *67 or simply use a calling card. You may want to have a family member or friend make the call in case the person answering the phone turns out to be someone you know. You may want to purchase a voice changer for $39.95 in case the person answering the phone turns out to be someone you know.

- Employ a script or pretext: See two time-tested choices in Chapter 3. If the number is unpublished, use the Alaskan Operator Pretext (page 72). If it is a cell phone number, use the Cell Phone Provider Pretext (page 73).

Sometimes, this is the only way to gather this essential information. No pretext is completely trouble-free, so you will want to be prepared for roadblocks. In the PI industry, we usually prepare for a pretext by doing a role-play with another agent, who will throw up questions. If you're uncomfortable doing a pretext yourself or your pretext fails, turn to a professional investigator.

Also be prepared for surprises. When I called the cell phone number planning to use the Alaskan pretext, the person who answered was Ginger, the wife of a local cardiologist, who was one of Randall's partners and Rita's best friend. Once I relayed this to Rita, she suddenly recalled that the scent on her husband's shirt the other night was White Diamonds—which Ginger, the bitch, always wore.

Cyberspy on E-mail Correspondence

If there are no unexplained repeated calls in the phone records, it's time to look for other forms of communication between the lovers, and e-mail is by far the most prevalent way sneaky lovers keep their romance hot and plan their trysts.

Use a Keystroke Recorder

Although it helps, you don't have to know how to turn on a computer or know your spouse's e-mail password to catch him or her setting up a dirty little assignation with the Buffy or Billy who is trying to steal your mate. With a simple device called a keystroke recorder, you can secure a printed record of every lover's mushy exchange and each electronic oooh and aaah, as well as the name of the motel.

The laws are always changing, so be sure you confirm that this type of surveillance is legal. You can purchase this secret storage device for $56 to $80 (available from www.tigerdirect.com, 1-800-800-8300). This baby is easier to plug in than a toaster and it goes right into your spouse's keyboard. This small, unobtrusive tubular device, 1 inch in length, simply attaches to the cheating bastard's keyboard cord. If your spouse has a laptop, you'll have to use the program, not the keystroke logger. Acting as a second hard drive (don't worry if you don't know what that is), it will record all keystrokes (anything written), incoming and outgoing—including those that are either romantic or x-rated—made by your spouse and his or her correspondents. This device will capture hundreds of pages of text; for the unskilled computer illiterate, this is a cheap and easy way to confirm your suspicions. Follow these steps to use a logger:

- Unplug the keyboard cord from the computer (if you don't know what that is, start at the keyboard and follow the cord to where it plugs into the computer).

- Plug the male connector of the keystroke logger into the female connector of the keyboard cord.

- Plug the keystroke device with the cord attached back into the computer.

- When your husband is out, remove the device and take it to a friend who can use a computer, or a computer shop that makes copies, such as Staples or Kinko's.

- Bring your paperwork with you that explains how to use the device.

- Read the correspondence for proof that he or she is or isn't having an affair.

- If the e-mails are steamy and incriminating, you've got not only your answer, but some hard evidence to wave in their lying mug—at the right time, of course.

- One important thing the keystroke logger does is capture your spouse's e-mail password, which can be employed in other ways.

If you are very computer literate, you can order a software program that must be installed on the computer's hard drive. The best keystroke recorder program is offered by Specter Pro (1-888-598-2788; or download the same program at www.spectpro.com). It costs about $99. You can also download a lesser product for free at www.keystrokefree.com. If you are downloading, save the program to a CD, which you then put on your husband's or wife's drive and follow the onscreen instructions. This program will reside on the hard drive—cloaked and undetectable—and will save an unlimited amount of data. Only you will be able to access this through the use of secret keys. Once you have the traitor's password, you can check their conversations all day long.

You Have the E-mail Address; Identify the Lover

The keystroke recorder confirmed it: Your husband or wife is definitely conducting a sexy e-mail exchange online, but you still don't know the name of the trollop or you're quite sure "Kitten" or "Stud" is not their Christian name. And their screen name is an anonymous: Gogo24@aol.com. You just know your spouse is boffing them with their keyboard every night. You have several choices here.

First, you can continue monitoring e-mails looking for a name, a phone number, or a meeting place and time where you can conduct physical surveillance and pull the lover's tag number. Search for any posting Kitten or Stud has made on the Internet by "googling" their e-mail address. To do this, go to google.com and type in the e-mail address and click the "Groups" tab. This will give you any posting Kitten or Stud has made about themselves or any topic about which they've commented. While this may not give you his or her name, it's a starting point. Using a pretext, e-mail Kitten or Stud, saying you saw their posting in a group—i.e., the orchid-lover's group or the poodle-owner's chat room. Make up a fictitious screen name. Attempt to engage them in a screen conversation. Carefully extract enough information to find out the real name of the target. For a recent client, I was able to identify his wife's cyberlover by striking up an e-mail correspondence with the

Internet lover once I had traced him to a cybergroup for men having hair replacement. I said I was going bald, and wanted his advice. He took the bait and I nailed him.

Should these methods fail to produce the name of this cyberslut or cyberstud, the easiest method for determining the name and address of your spouse's e-mail lover is to pay a local PI to convert the e-mail account into a real name and address. The average cost is about $200.

Use GPS Surveillance

If there are no phone records and no e-mail correspondence, it's time for surveillance. However, with a cheap cell phone or a more expensive GPS tracker and the high-tech capabilities of GPS, you can conduct physical surveillance without leaving home. You can follow your husband's or wife's daily movements from sunrise to sunset—every strange address, every trip to the men's room, every flower shop, every motel—without ever getting up from your computer desk.

GPS-Enabled Cell Phone

You can purchase a GPS-enabled cell phone for roughly $79 at Wal-Mart and buy $20 worth of minutes to make the cell phone operational. After purchasing the phone, take the following steps:

- Subscribe to a GPS locator service (www.ulocate.com or call 1-800-666-5782) which costs $12.95 per month; all of the phone companies are in the process of adding this feature for a minimal charge to the basic package.

- Charge the phone and plant it on your husband's or wife's person, in their vehicle, or give it to them as a gift (this is the best choice for dependable reception).

- If going the covert route, turn off the ringer and place it covertly in the vehicle somewhere in the passenger compartment—for example, under the rear passenger seat. (Reception may be a bit compromised, but you can count on 90 percent surveillance. Remove it and recharge it every two days while they're sleeping).

Once planted, you can log on to ulocate.com and enter the phone number. You can look up the immediate location, which tells you where the cell phone and your spouse are at that moment (a map will appear pinpointing the bastard's location within thirty feet at that moment). You can also request a location history, which tells you where the cell phone and the car have been for as long as you've been conducting this surveillance. You can print the map that appears on screen, then highlight a location on the map and click the link to Mapquest, which will give you the exact address where your husband or wife has parked their car, and possibly their fidelity.

Use a GPS Tracker

You can go high-tech with a GPS tracking device to conduct your surveillance—as long as you own the vehicle involved. For $295.00, you can buy and attach a GPS tracker to your vehicle, in this case your spouse's. The tracker is about the size of a Walkman radio and runs on size-A batteries. It will run for more than a week on one set. You then recover the unit, attach it to your computer, and download the data. Using mapping software, you will then know every address the vehicle stopped at, the date, and how long it stayed at one place. One such tracker is available at www.vehicletracking.com/products/3100.html. It's like having a private investigator for a fraction of the cost. It can be attached almost anywhere on the car or in the car and is self-contained. No wiring or installation is involved.

You Have an Address: Identify the Homewrecker

If you find your husband or wife, their new cell phone, and their car making daily or weekly visits to an unexplained physical address, it's time to look for a name.

- Go to www.freeality.com/finde.htm, click on Search by Address and you will see a name and phone number of the person listed at that address.

- Go to the library, where you can use the reverse-address section of one of the many city directories available in your public library.

- The tax collector's office will also release the name of the property owner if you provide the address.

- The lover may be renting so be careful not to link your spouse mistakenly to their lover's landlord.

If the above fails, a local PI should only charge about $20 to convert your address to a name.

Conducting Physical Surveillance

Suppose phone records, Internet sleuthing, and covert cell phone surveillance have not produced any proof that your spouse has a lover. Either they've covered their tracks or they're innocent. But you're not ready to give up. They're still staring off into space and have just bought you an expensive gift for no reason. You just want the truth. To be absolutely sure that the gift meant "I love you" and that the "lover" is all in your imagination, you can resort to one final option—follow them.

You've pinpointed the suspicious hours in your spouse's day during which he or she is in some vague location and usually can't be reached. This may be the early morning hours before work when they are allegedly running eight miles or, as in the case of Rita's husband, making rounds at the hospital. Now follow them. You may not actually catch them red-handed, but you will find out if they're lying about where they go and you'll have an address if they stop at a strange location. What follows are the typical steps professionals follow for infidelity surveillance, steps you can take yourself.

Preparation

Before you even think about attempting to tail your spouse, read Chapter 7 first. Using the techniques in this chapter, make the necessary preparations to your car, gather your spyware and props, and study relevant surveillance tactics before attempting to tail your mark.

Assemble Equipment

In order to conduct a basic surveillance, you'll need:

- **A pair of cheap binoculars that can fold up and be hidden in your pocket.**

- **A car that won't be recognized by your better half. This can be borrowed from a friend or rented.**

- **A simple disguise, using a baseball hat and sunglasses, that will keep you from being identified. Tuck your hair up under the cap.**

- **A sunscreen for the windshield with a small hole in it, in case you are going to conduct a stakeout. That way, no one will know there's a person in the car, but you can be watching the building.**

Buy Time with a Pretext

Ask your spouse to do an errand on the way to work at a specific drug store or business. Then, drive to that destination and pick up the trail there. This gives you a chance to get your covert vehicle moving without the mark seeing you follow them directly from home.

Find their car in the parking lot of the drug store or errand destination. Park 100 feet away or more and wait for him or her to leave. Sit patiently until a car is between you and your spouse and then pull out, heading in the same direction. Follow the directions for tailing a mark outlined in Chapter 7.

When I began tailing Randall, I soon realized he was heading in the opposite direction from the hospital where he was supposed to be doing his morning rounds. He hadn't been doing rounds at all during the early morning—he'd been doing Ginger. From my vantage point of two car lengths back, I wondered where the bastard was going. Ginger was married to Randall's partner—surely he wasn't going to their house! I wouldn't think he'd be that dumb, but then, I've seen it all in twenty-two years. If he did go there, it would make my job a whole lot easier, but I figured him to be smarter than that and that he'd choose to meet somewhere neutral and less risky.

Residential Location

If your spouse pulls onto the street or into a driveway of a house, condo, or apartment complex, continue on by, turn in a driveway, and head back in the opposite direction, parking at least 300 feet away. If you haven't made the proper preparations for a stakeout (hey, you were hoping the jerk was innocent), hang out long enough to get the street address of the residence your future ex just entered and blow out of there.

However, if you're undetected and can wait it out, write down the numbers from any cars in the driveway or parked on the street, and any other information about this destination. If you can wait long enough, observe the spouse's exit to see if the two-timing cheater kisses someone goodbye at the door or sneaks out looking over a shoulder. Is there someone watching from the door, waving goodbye, or discreetly pulling aside a curtain? Even if you don't see your spouse actually embrace another person, you have the address of someone your partner visits on the way to work.

As I had guessed, Randall didn't go to a residential location, which would have been his partner's house. I continued to stay two and three car lengths back, wondering if he was headed for some secret lover's early morning hideaway. But he didn't go to a motel or a secret hideout. Instead, he went to Starbucks.

Commercial Destination

Hey, what's this? Your spouse stops at a coffee shop instead of going to work or the gym. You made them coffee that morning. And offered a fresh bagel, which they refused. Often, when there are no traceable forms of communication, the cheating couple arranges to rendezvous in person, usually in a public setting. Here's what you should do if this happens:

- Park in commercial setting to blend in.

- Wait, using the pretext of looking at a map or reading the paper.

- Observe the entrance and note single customers who enter soon after your spouse. If you don't know the identity of the lover, watch for a customer entering alone who seems in a hurry and looking for someone. If you do know the identity of the lover (or have a suspicion) and that person appears, don't blow your cover by jumping out of your car and confronting the homewrecker.

- Observe the exit. Is someone with your spouse as he or she exits? Who leaves immediately afterwards? Does the person who entered after your spouse exit at the same time?

I parked in the middle of the lot, near a lot of other cars, with a clear view of the Starbucks entrance, and waited. Within a few minutes, Ginger, who I recognized from a snapshot Rita had given me, bounced into Starbucks. Unless they were planning a surprise birthday party for Ginger's husband, Rita's best friend and husband were conducting their affair right out in public over café latte. As I watched through my binoculars, Randall walked Ginger to her car, and his innocent goodbye kiss suddenly turned into a hot, groping embrace—he even reached under Ginger's skirt and copped a quick feel. Okay, so much for the birthday party theory. But now I needed some solid proof.

If You Don't Recognize or Know the Lover

Now, I knew who to look for because Rita had provided me with a photo once we determined it was Ginger behind the cell phone number. But chances are you may not know the face of your rival. If you don't know, watch for your spouse to leave. Usually a couple conducting an affair will say farewell outside the establishment where they met. The male half of the duo will often walk the female to her car where a good-bye embrace takes place. Next, follow these steps:

- Follow the lover's movements during the rest of the day; it's a good guess they arranged a later meeting to finish what they started in the public parking lot.

- Follow the usurper to a place of work or a residential location.

- Get the lover's license plate number.

- If the lover goes home, get the address.

Now that you have an address and the license plate numbers of the cars near the house where your spouse spent a secret hour, you're ready to find out the name of the sleazeball who's bonking them. If you want to use the address, follow the steps outlined under the heading, You Have an Address: Identify the Homewrecker, on page 21.

If you have the license plate number, you can go to the local tax collector's office in the county that issues new license tags and fill out a request form for identifying the owner of a license plate (laws vary from state to state, so you may not be able to obtain this information in your area).

How Long Should You Investigate?

How long should you continue your investigation if there's no immediate, clear indication that your spouse is cheating? Suppose you've put in two weeks of heavy sleuthing and found nothing incriminating. Is it safe to assume your spouse is an angel, not a devil? Were those suspicions just your imagination gone wild? Without actual proof that there is a lover, you need to be patient. How long depends on how careful the creep is. Before you rest easy, give it a third week by continuing with phone, e-mail, and electronic surveillance. Continue driving by the home or coffee shop in the morning to establish if this is a pattern. Above all, act as normal as possible and don't get caught.

For one thing, the meetings you've been observing at the coffee shop could be legitimate. If your spouse ends up in the clear, you'd rather your beloved didn't know about your binoculars and the GPS cell phone you planted under the back seat of your mate's car.

Or has your wily spouse read Chapter 2 of this book and covered his or her tracks? Although it took me only three days going through cell phone records and a trip to Starbucks to establish that Randall was two-timing Rita with Ginger, each case is different. Sometimes, it takes me anywhere from one phone call to a two-week stakeout to establish the truth.

Don't Confront the Two-Timer with Your Proof

Yes, you know your spouse is cheating and you now know with whom. But all you have is a name and an address and, perhaps, some sightings. It's critical that you resist the overwhelming temptation to confront the cheating bastard. You just risk tipping your hand and sending the cheater underground.

Confronting the two-timer with a name you pulled from a license plate tag and some cell phone records is dangerously premature. These documents may not be adequate bargaining chips to get the financial and custody separation agreement you want. Against my advice, one of my clients—let's call her Mary—waved the name and phone record of calls to "Buffy" in her husband's face. He insisted that Buffy was just a "friend" who was consoling him about his problems at work, just a colleague who he contacted frequently by phone and e-mail. Mary's conversation went like this: "So, how come I never met her or heard her name before?" to which Mary's husband replied, "Because I knew you'd react like this." Alerted, Mary's husband went into protective mode, and she eventually had to pay my firm several thousand more dollars in surveillance costs to secure the video footage she needed (Buffy was definitely doing much more than listening). She would have gotten proof much more quickly and cheaply had she reined in her anger and been patient.

What you must do is keep your cool. Once you've established that your spouse is meeting someone else, and you've followed the tramp or the gigolo long enough to get data for identification, calm down, go home, and prepare.

That's what I needed to do. We needed positive proof for Rita's lawyer and the judge (if they were going to divorce, and it certainly looked that way at this point) that Randall and Ginger were playing doctor/nurse. If you are going to do this, you'll need to keep your emotions in check. For starters, read the relevant chapters in this book, collect the needed spyware, and disguise your vehicle for a stakeout. Focus on collecting legally solid evidence that would be kickass bargaining chips for alimony, child custody, and humiliation.

NAIL THE BASTARD WITH HARD EVIDENCE

YOU MAY HAVE witnessed a kiss in the doorway or watched your partner's car in the driveway of her trainer's apartment for two hours when she was supposed to be playing bridge. But it's still your word against theirs. Randall and Ginger could still claim that the phone contact and the meeting at Starbucks was innocent. Rita needed legal ammunition to clean Randall's clock. She had, after all, two children to protect. And a score to settle.

In Rita's example, we knew that Randall was meeting Ginger casually, but didn't know where they actually went to cheat. To collect evidence that will make your mate incontinent before a judge, you need pictures, a surveillance log, names and addresses, and possibly a video.

If you know they meet at the lover's house, then move on to the section below titled Shadow the Lover to the Rendezvous. But if you don't know the lover's address, or you do but don't know if they do the nasty at that locale, you may want to run a full or partial intelligence report on the woman or man who's moving in on your territory (see Chapter 3). In addition to the lover's address and daily route for shadowing purposes, an intelligence report could contain many clues to the love nest. A check online of property records may show that the slut owns a beach house or a condo.

We ran a report on Ginger and discovered that Rita's now ex–best friend and soon-to-be-ex-husband's lover owned an upscale motel. This was obviously where Randall was playing around with Ginger.

Shadow the Lover to the Rendezvous

Your spouse and lover hopefully don't know you're on to them, so while your spouse may be on the lookout, the lover may be moving about freely. Freely enough for you to follow the lover's trail undetected and nail both of their asses at the secret meeting place. But make sure you review the shadowing, tailing, and fixed surveillance tactics in Chapter 7. You'll never get those photos and video footage if the cheaters make you and they take a breather.

Follow the lover from work during the hours when your mate is mysteriously occupied. Bingo. You're probably driving by the motel as your mate is looking over his shoulder on the way into the motel room. You have a location and a time.

I had followed Randall enough to know he met Ginger two mornings a week at Starbuck's, but three mornings a week they were clearly getting laid rather than getting latte.

Get Photographic Evidence

If you don't have damning photos or videotapes, your cheating husband or wife will continue to claim they are "just friends." It's "he said/she said" about what you saw. What can't be refuted is a 3-minute movie of the father or mother of your children making out like a teenager in a Chevy in the corner of a parking lot.

You can collect two kinds of photographic evidence: footage of the two slimeballs meeting and holding hands in a public place proving contact; and/or, the grand slam, photos of the guilty duo entering and leaving a motel. Thus, you'll be assuming a stakeout at the public meeting place in your parked car where you have observed the lover's meeting to talk and to plan: a coffee shop, a house, a cabin in the woods, a park. Hopefully, you can also get footage set up in the primary position you staked out at a residence or motel.

To win at the negotiating table, you need raw footage of ass patting, breast fondling—or the big mama of them all, a videotape of Miss Buffy giving the jerk a blow job in broad daylight. With such footage, one of my clients cleaned her husband's clock. She got almost everything. Her husband was a federal employee—a twenty-year man—whose agency had a strict policy about interoffice affairs. If you got caught screwing with a fellow employee, you were history and so was your retirement. She used my video footage—which I got from my vantage point up in a tree—as a bargaining chip to get the joint property in both states and a handsome alimony check each month.

Preparation

Review Chapter 7, under the heading Electronic Video Surveillance: Nanny Cams and Hidden Cameras, page 215, to help you prepare for taping. Assemble the needed equipment (See Appendix 2). You will need:

- A camcorder. Although you should bring camera as a backup, one minute of videotape is the equivalent of 500 still photographs.

- A backup still camera. The preferred is a 35mm with a 200mm zoom (I always have my agents bring a camera in case the video camera fails).

- Basic stakeout paraphernalia such as a hat, sunglasses, a sunshade, and an unrecognizable vehicle.

Videotaping at a Public Venue

If you find yourself having to tape outside a motel, restaurant, or other public place, assume a stakeout position that offers a view of the door through which the jerk will exit and an open view of the parking lot. I knew Ginger's car and had the door to Starbucks and Ginger's Mustang convertible in my camcorder's lens.

Then, slip a paper bag with a hole over the video camera and begin shooting your mark as they exit. If they leave alone, keep the video camera pointed at the entrance. Get footage of any lone woman or man leaving soon after the mark and videotape them walking to the parking lot until he or she either leaves alone or meets up with your spouse.

If you have a cell phone number from your earlier detection efforts, dial *67 to block your ID and dial his or her number to see if they begin to grope for the phone. Keep taping in case they meet in the parking lot, where you can possibly get footage of some further groping.

Knowing that Randall could easily claim he was "just friends" with Ginger (his "partner's wife"), I prepared to shoot some footage of Randall and Ginger in a post-latte, pre-coital clutch. Over a ten-day period, I was able to collect four different mini-movies of Randall almost doing the dirty with Ginger in the Starbucks parking lot.

Videotaping at a Residence

If you need to tape outside a residence, get a stakeout position in your car so you have a good view of the doorway through which your spouse will exit. Slip a paper bag with a hole over the video camera. As the door to the house or apartment complex opens, start the camcorder running immediately. You may have only five seconds to get the goods. There may only be a goodbye embrace in a doorway, an identifiable image of the homewrecker for court, an image from which to print a still shot for further identification if you don't know the lover, or even some partial nudity at noon—in which case, your picture could be worth several thousand dollars.

Although Randall and Ginger were careful, after two weeks of watching the motel room near where Randall's car was parked, I got a shot of the chump Rita married tongue-kissing Ginger in the doorway of one of the rooms at Ginger's motel. When Rita's attorney eventually gave copies to Randall's lawyer, a settlement offer was forthcoming. Neither Ginger nor Randall wanted the tapes to become public record.

Continue your videotaping sessions until you have at least three compromising tapes. One would be sufficient, but three proves it's an ongoing relationship.

Finding Secret Gifts

The size of your alimony payment can hinge on whether the cheater is spending big bucks on the third leg of the triangle. It's critical to find out. To look for gifts that were intended for someone other than you, you'll need your spouse's personal and/or corporate credit-card numbers, which you can secure from a bill or from the card itself that you pulled from their wallet while they were otherwise preoccupied. Also, be prepared with a fax number where you can have faxed copies of statements sent. Then use a pretext call to the credit card provider to investigate whether there have been any unexplained, secret, or suspicious purchases.

If You Have the Credit Card Bill

Employ a pretext with the credit card company. Claim to be your spouse's secretary or business manager and request clarification about all charges to retail stores. Tell them you need this to properly assign charges to the appropriate partners who use the account.

Or, use a voice changer or a gender-appropriate friend and claim to be the card holder. Make sure you request clarification about "unexplained charges" to retail stores; "I'm afraid my teenage son is using my card." "I believe there is a mistake on my bill; I don't remember making these purchases." Then, request the actual items purchased from these stores.

If You Have the Personal Credit Card Number, but No Bill

Employ a pretext with the credit card provider. Use a voice changer or a gender-appropriate friend and claim to be the card holder, and improvise on the following script:

YOU (pretending to be your spouse): I have a question about my last bill. I'm certain that I hadn't charged that much. I don't know if my teenage son has been using my card. Anyway, I've misplaced my bill, but I need to know what was on it. Can you help me?

CUSTOMER SERVICE: Sure. First, may I have your billing address and social security number? (The mother's maiden name and pet's name may be needed here.)

YOU (responding to a charge to a jewelry store or department store): I don't remember shopping there. What were the actual items purchased?

CUSTOMER SERVICE: Will that be all?

YOU: Is there any chance you could fax me a copy?

CUSTOMER SERVICE: Sure. Can I have the fax number?

If a customer service operator balks, wait ten minutes and call back until you get an operator who is more cooperative.

If You Have a Corporate Card Number, but No Bill

If you have your spouse's corporate credit card number, but no bill, you will first need to secure the corporate FEIN number for your spouse's workplace. To do this:

- Go to www.publicrecordsfinder.com.

- Click on **Search the 50 States**.

- Click on your state.

- Click on **Corporations** to go to the corporations database.

- Enter the corporation name and the FEIN number for most corporations will appear.

Once you have the number, improvise on the following pretext with the card company.

YOU: Hello, I'm calling for Medical Park Group in Somewhere, Ohio (your husband's workplace). There was a problem with the charges, but I misplaced the last bill. It's my job to post these charges to the appropriate partners and I never straightened the charges at my end. Could you go over them with me, please?

CUSTOMER SERVICE: Hi, I'm Gina. I'm sorry you're having trouble. I need some information.

YOU: (Provide requested identification information: usually corporate name, address, and FEIN number.)

CUSTOMER SERVICE: Let's start at the top. There is a charge at Saks Fifth Avenue for $167.80.

YOU: I don't recognize that charge. That must be where the error is. No one here would be charging something at a department store. The item?

CUSTOMER SERVICE: Ladies' lingerie. A negligee and robe.

YOU: Oh. One of the doctors must have gotten that as a surprise for his wife. Thank you. I want to be sure, though, and ask the partners about it. Is there any chance you could fax me a copy?

CUSTOMER SERVICE: Of course. Can I have the fax number, please?

Unfortunately, you never received the heart-shaped diamond charm, the silk teddy, or the flowers that your husband has been purchasing for the past six months. But someone did. Even if customer service refuses to fax a copy, you know the proof exists and you can always have your lawyer subpoena the records. These gifts can be critical evidence in a negotiating session or before a judge.

Collect Witness Affidavits

If possible, obtain written statements or affidavits from one or more witnesses who can confirm the existence of the affair. For the amateur private eye, a legal, written statement is usually too difficult to obtain. If you succeed, you're either very lucky or very talented. But it's worth a try. These are important because a number of things can happen between the day you first catch Mr. Cheater and Miss Buffy and when you have your day in court. Potential witnesses include: friends, relatives, coworkers, neighbors, cashiers, retail clerks, parking lot attendants, doormen, waitresses, maître d's, pool boys, landscapers, handymen, housekeepers, baby-sitters, and/or motel clerks. A time-sensitive, signed witness statement about the details of the relationship will serve several purposes:

- **Help a witness prepare for testifying so many months after the events (sometimes as much as six months to a year).**

- Act as a safeguard against a subpoenaed witness changing his or her testimony.

- Challenge a witness who changes a story or forgets some details.

In Rita's case, I found a credit card receipt for a silk teddy which she had never received. I gave it to her, and she put it into a safe deposit box until she was ready to meet with her attorney. But in order to really seal the deal, we went after some X-rated footage. Rita wanted revenge—to humiliate and subdue her soon-to-be ex with a witness.

Proper Legal Procedure for an Affidavit

If the affidavit is written or typed, it must be notarized (most PIs and their operatives are notary publics), so plan ahead for that. An audio- or videotaped affidavit must contain the:

- date and location,

- the witness's name, address, and profession, and

- a statement whereby the witness acknowledges that the conversation is being taped and giving permission to tape the interview.

If you can't remember what to include, make a cheat sheet of notes on what to ask or what information to obtain. Now you're ready to conduct the interview.

- Identify yourself.

- Ask for the parking attendant's or motel clerk's name. (Even if the potential witness says no, you'll need a name if you want to subpoena him or her later.)

- Get as many details as possible before you reveal you're collecting legal evidence.

- Explain that you want the person's help.

- Reveal your relationship to the cheater.

- Tell your story of woe—briefly.

- Appeal to the witness's sense of justice.

- Appeal to the witness's empathy.

- Be completely honest.

Here's a sample script you can improvise on to illustrate the above.

YOU: Hello, my name is _____ (your real name) and I'm hoping you'll be willing to help me. (Begin to cry.) I have two young children whose future could be in your hands.

PARKING VALET: What do you mean? I don't even know you.

YOU: I know. I'm sorry. All I'm asking you to do is tell the truth. Do you know Dr. _____? He drives a green Jaguar.

PARKING VALET: Oh sure, I know him. He always tips me five bucks.

YOU: I saw him with a redhead yesterday, and I just want to know if they come here all the time.

PARKING VALET: Gee. I always thought that was his wife or girlfriend. I didn't know he was married.

YOU: (Begin to cry.) He's married with two little children. I can't believe this is happening to me.

PARKING VALET: I'm not sure how I can help.

YOU: Have you ever had a girlfriend or wife cheat on you?

PARKING VALET: Well, yes.

YOU: You remember how bad that made you feel? I just need to know what's happening. I feel like such a fool. How often do they come here?

PARKING VALET: About three times a week. He always walks her to her car.

YOU: Do they kiss?

PARKING VALET: Well, yes. I remember he gave her some roses one day.

YOU: Roses? He hasn't given me flowers since our second child was born. (Begin to weep.) Please help me.

PARKING VALET: Look, I don't know if I should be talking to you. I don't really want to get involved.

YOU: I'm only asking you to tell the truth. Remember how it felt to be betrayed? (Continue to weep.)

PARKING VALET: Well, what do you want me to do?

YOU: (Whip out the pictures of your two sons.) You've already told me what you saw. I just want to have it on tape. This isn't for court. It's for my attorney. It's just another piece of proof that it's true. I'm not sure my attorney even believes me.

PARKING VALET: Well, I don't know.

YOU: (Punch the Record button on the tape recorder and pull out your cheat sheet.) For this tape to be legal I have to ask you two questions at the beginning of the tape.

YOU: (Speak into the tape.) This is May 21, 2004 at the downtown Marriot Hotel parking garage. John Jones, you're aware

I'm recording this conversation? Could you please state your name and profession. How long have you been doing this? Do you agree to answer a few questions on tape and just tell the truth about what you saw?

Because you've had an informal conversation first, you already know what the witness knows and what facts you want in the affidavit (on the tape), so you prompt the witness to repeat this information with questions.

> **YOU**: (Step closer.) So you told me that you've seen Dr. Smith here in the parking garage with a redheaded woman. Is this her? (Show him her picture.) Who did you think she was? Tell me about the roses. Estimate how long you've seen them coming here. What did you think their relationship was? How often did you see them kiss? Did you see them do anything else intimate?

Once you have conducted all interviews, preserve the tapes for later use. Label each tape with the date, time, and your initials (it may be six months from this time that it will actually be produced as evidence, and you'll be expected to name the time and place you took the footage). If the witness is going to testify in court, mail a copy of the written affidavit or videotape to the witness a few days before he or she is scheduled to testify. This guarantees that all recollections will be detailed and accurate.

Legally Preserve All Physical Evidence

Suppose you've gotten a hold of the lover's panties and placed them in a paper bag. Now you want to have them tested, so you can dangle them before the judge with the lab results attached when that cheating Jezebel tries to deny you alimony. At least that's what Rita wanted to do. The final straw in Rita's mind was a salmon-colored thong Ginger left under the back seat of Randall's car.

At this point, I usually collect a check for semen testing, and send off the panties with $500 to $600 dollars to a lab that will give me a written report. I charge another $500 for my efforts. But don't pay me. I told Rita not to. Like Rita, you can save yourself $500 and maybe $1,000 by buying a $59.95 semen test kit from Chambers Investigations, 606 49th St. West, Bradenton, FL 34209. With a home test, you can verify that the stain is evidence of infidelity before you spend the $500 to verify it through any number of private labs listed on the Internet (See www.chambersagency.com).

Evidence that has been legally obtained and preserved for your attorney to use in court is critical for every investigation. Every case hinges on the best proof you can gather. This holds true even if you don't go to court. Oftentimes, evidence—for example, panties in a baggie without a lab report—will be all the leverage you need to settle a civil case in your favor.

So, in Rita's case, I collected receipts, e-mail correspondence, a pair of panties, an embarrassingly mushy Hallmark card, credit card bills, video footage of her spouse doing some X-rated groping in a parking lot, and videotapes of witness statements.

It's essential that you correctly preserve the chain of evidence for each item or it will be challenged. You want solid evidence aimed at the heart and/or pocketbook of your ex. Follow carefully the standard methods outlined in Appendix One including correctly documenting the source of evidence, maintaining the chain of evidence (remember O. J.'s infamous glove), and correctly storing evidence in a locked secured area (refrigerated where appropriate) to which only you or your attorney have a key. Otherwise, your evidence will be challenged.

Now, you've got the ammunition you need to get everything you want in an out-of-court negotiating session with your lawyers. When you slap down the photos, pop in the footage, and produce the affidavits, it's your spouse's worse nightmare. Your ex will likely fold. It's payback for the pain, rejection, and anxiety you've been suffering since the person you loved gave all of their time, love, and money to someone else. The kids are yours, the check is bigger, and your ex is humiliated.

Rita walked out with everything but Randall's medical degree, including the resources and the determination to go back to school herself. She also got the pleasure of knowing that Ginger dumped the newly impoverished Randall just before Ginger's husband booted her out on her ass. The last she heard they were both alone, miserable, and broke.

COVER YOUR ASS

YOU SHUT OFF the car and walk toward your front door, wondering what the hell is going on. In the moonlight, you can just make out your golf clubs, business suits, and assorted clothes strewn all over the front yard. You try your key, but the chain is on the door. It's 1:00 a.m. and you'd meant to enter quietly without waking anyone.

"You no good piece of goat filth!" calls your wife from the other side of the door. "I am taking the children, the house and the business." She then shoves three 8 × 10 glossies through the mail slot in the door. It's you and the product rep making out in front of a motel door. You want a stiff drink. You want to shrink to the size of dust mite.

Because you didn't take precautions, you, my friend, are screwed. You're nailed and, I'm sorry to say, the divorce summons ain't far behind. Consider the following statistics:

- **Percentage of married men and women who cheat: 60**

- **Percentage of spouses who report their marriages were improved by an affair: 59**

- Percentage of couples who stayed married after an affair is revealed: 76

- Percentage of men who say they tell no one about their mates' affair: 24

- Percentage of wronged spouses who want every detail of their partner's affair: 62

- Percentage of cheating men who have more than one affair: 66

- Average number of affairs for women who cheat: 1 to 3

- Percentage of affluent men having extramarital sex while married: 75

- Percentage of cheating partners who have transmitted an STD to their mate: 25

- Cost of hiring me for advice on how to cover your ass: $200

- Cost of covering your own ass: $0

Of course, having your golf clubs tossed on the lawn could have been prevented. If you cheat like 60 percent of all Americans—and infidelity has been at the heart of over half of the 20,000 cases I have worked on during my career—you can increase your chances of getting away with it if you do things by the book. *This* book.

People have many reasons for engaging in infidelity. I don't encourage or endorse it, but I don't judge people, either. I know preachers, politicians, bakers—people from all walks of life—who've cheated. No one is immune to becoming lonely and fewer still are immune to sexual chemistry. They're just like you, perhaps trying to scratch that deep-rooted itch for love, romance, danger, excitement, affection, or a good screw. For some, it's acting on a one-time urge, for others, it's payback, and for some, like "Mary," you just want to follow your heart three times a week for a few hours in a motel and not get caught. Mary had been sleeping with her roofing contractor "Joe," and now the roof was done, but not the affair. Even as the last shingle had been laid—well, you get the idea. But she didn't want a divorce, either. She loved her impotent, older husband and the father of her teenage children. She liked her life and didn't want to hurt her spouse. Or get detected. Like all cheating spouses, she wanted to have sex without getting caught. That's where this chapter comes in. Weeping into a tissue as she sat in my office, she described Joe as a sweet guy and a true southern gentleman, even if he wasn't quite thirty years old.

I told Mary, as I tell all my clients looking to cheat, that she should consider the risks and truly decide if the affair is worth it. And, if she still wanted to go forward, then she needed to follow some ground rules to prevent getting caught by her spouse or a PI he's hired. I'm a social engineer who's seen and heard it all as I tracked down cheating spouses. The few who outsmarted me and covered their asses were employing the techniques I share here. What you do with the information is purely your call.

Some clients come to me for advice on avoiding detection before beginning the affair, but most show up when the indiscretion is underway and they have reason to fear their spouse is suspicious. I don't promise that you won't get caught if you use the tactics described in this chapter, but I can help you drastically cut the odds. You'll stand a much better chance of not being in that embarrassing position of seeing the 8×10 glossies waved about the courtroom as you slink further down into your chair—all under the biblical, contemptuous stare of the judge.

So, read this chapter before all your stuff ends up on the lawn, and you may just be able to save your ass. Now, clean that lipstick off your collar and sit down. You and I are about to have a heart to heart.

CALCULATE THE RISKS

SO, YOU WANT to cheat, eh? Before you do, look in the mirror and tell yourself the truth, which is the first thing I make every client tell me. If you want me to help you, you need to be perfectly honest. And, since you've hired yourself, you need to level with yourself. Look at the odds you'll get caught and look at the risks. That means, before beginning an affair or continuing one, ask yourself the question I always asked: Is it worth it? Of course, you may just skip this section.

Cheating on a spouse requires cunning, motivation, clarity of purpose, and an understanding of the consequences to join the ranks of the slim minority that are completely successful. The following odds are not based on scientific surveys or statistical calculations; they're based on my observations over twenty-two years of fidelity work. And common sense.

The Best Odds: A One-Night Stand

A one-time fling is easier to get away with than a regular thing. It ain't love, but your chances of getting caught are slim. If you continue to meet with the lover, you're betting against the house. The more times you meet with the lover, the more the odds increase that you'll get caught. But if you don't repeat it and behave normally at home, your chances are good. You made a mistake. You're sorry. It's over. Even if your mate suspects you've bonked someone, he or she may not try to find out about what they don't want to know.

Poor Odds: A Regular Thing

The average odds of getting caught having a long affair are about 70 percent. You can trim that down by keeping the fling short term and following some guidelines in this chapter. The longer the affair, the more telltale evidence there will be, and it's only a matter of time until your mate stumbles across something you cannot explain. It could be as simple as the lover's phone number on your cell display, or worse yet, a friend who sees you two together at the hot sheet motel and rats you out. Because nothing is a sure thing, you might want to have an overnight bag packed.

Multiple Flings: You're Toast

If you make cheating a regular thing, it is never a question of "if" but "when" it will catch up with you. And when the train wreck happens, it will not be a Kodak moment. If you're reckless in love, chances are you're reckless when it comes to covering your ass. Keep your suitcase packed, and your attorney's phone number on your speed dial.

Are the Consequences Worth It?

The first question I have for anyone thinking about having an affair is this: Is it worth the risks? Think about the consequences. I've seen cheating spouses lose everything. Once I feel a potential cheater is being honest, I ask him or her to think it over. I'm not your judge, but have you considered all the risks? Are you willing to throw away your twenty-five-year marriage for a roll in the hay?

So, before you consider an extramarital affair, always consider the possibility that you will be detected and ask yourself the same things I ask my clients:

- **Can you handle the financial repercussions? (Divorces are usually financially devastating for everyone but the attorneys. You could lose everything.)**

- **Can you handle the custody repercussions?**

- **How trustworthy is the love object? How well do you know him or her? (You take a chance when you play with a lover who doesn't have as much to lose as you do.)**

- **Is the lover married to an insanely jealous maniac?**

- **Is the lover possessive, vindictive, or unstable?**

- Are you willing to risk hurting the lover? (If you get caught, the lover usually does too; the lawyer for the wronged spouse can subpoena the lover anyway and ask all number of embarrassing questions, especially if the lover is married.)

- How are your acting skills? You will be leading a double life, and displaying two personalities.

- Do you have the emotional resources to cheat? Can you handle the guilt and humiliation?

- Do you have the financial resources? (If you're male, you're keeping two women happy, and that ain't cheap.)

- Are you willing to risk your health as well as your spouse's?

And, you need to examine your actual motives for wanting an affair in the first place. Is it because of low self-esteem, pity, lust, or true love? Are you doing it for fun (a "sport fuck") or for revenge (a "spite fuck")?

The spite fuck has few rewards. "Tricia L" asked me for advice about screwing her husband's best friend. She was contemplating responding to the friend's long-time advances because her husband was cheating on her. I knew, because I'd caught him for her.

After we talked, she realized that if she got caught (and what else was the point of a revenge screw?), she would lose the high-ground advantage in any settlement, in court, or even if the marriage continued. As she used up a half a box of tissues in our emotional conversation, she admitted that she was still hoping to reconcile with her husband. She wasn't in love with the husband's friend. She didn't even like him that much, especially because the creep had been coming on to her for years. She paid me for my time and left my office, ready to tell her husband's disloyal friend to go fuck himself.

Screw the Risk

Okay, let's say your situation is different. It's not a spite fuck, you're actually in love. Or it's just a great sport fuck that you just can't pass up. Or maybe, you've been neglected by your spouse for so long, and you just want some companionship. That was Mary's reason. And maybe, like her, you don't care about the risks. Nothing matters but being with that other person. Okay, well, if you're going to do it, then let's do it right.

DETERMINE IF YOU'RE UNDER SUSPICION

MAYBE YOU'RE ONLY on first base with your affair, but negotiations are underway, and you wonder if your spouse senses the impending indiscretion. Or, maybe you've already done the deed, and you're afraid your mate suspects something. "Betsy" came to me after the fact. While the ink was drying on her separation agreement, Betsy had gotten drunk and taken out her hostilities against the jerk she was divorcing, engaging in a spite fuck with a virtual stranger. Now, she wanted to cover it up. After a very emotional conversation and another box of tissues, she was crying "I didn't want to do it. I don't want to get caught." Does your mate suspect you? Let's find out.

Look For Red Flags

Unless your mate has read Chapter 1 and/or is an excellent actor, you should be able to pick up those subtle changes on the home front—the signs that your spouse is suspicious:

- Has anything been moved on a desk, in the car, in a closet, in a clothing drawer, in a purse, in a bedside table? Mary suspected her panties had been refolded. One day, she came out of the shower to find that the cell phone she'd left on her dresser was now on the coffee table.

- Is your spouse's behavior altered? Is he or she suddenly more possessive, affectionate, sexually attentive, cool, or moody? It doesn't matter what the changed behavior is; what matters is that there's a change. A spouse doesn't become overly possessive without a catalyst. Is your mate asking new questions and introducing new and unexpected lines of conversation?

- Is your mate engaging in unexplained activities? Mary knew she was under surveillance when she caught her husband checking the mileage on her car. He told her he was checking to see if she needed an oil change, which he'd never done before.

- Are you being followed? (See Chapters 7 and 8.)

- Has your computer been tampered with? Check for a keystroke recorder. Use a program to detect if a spy program secretly resides in your hard drive. You know you didn't put one there.

- Has your cell phone provider been contacted by someone claiming to be your secretary or you?

- Has your lover experienced anything suspicious, such as strange calls from a Canadian phone company or any other solicitation that could be a pretext to get a name and address? How about being tailed by a car or on foot? Did he/she notice any strangers pointing binoculars, cameras, or video cameras in their direction?

- Look for your mate's Internet trails. Using the arrow at the right of the site window, look down the list of recently visited sites. If one of them is Chambers Investigations, you've got a problem. Check your spouse's recent e-mail for correspondence with a PI.

ESTABLISH YOUR PRETEXTS

DON'T USE "WORKING late" or a "special project" as excuses for why you're missing from home. Those excuses usually send up red flags right away. Here are some pretexts you can use to disappear for a couple of hours a week.

Therapy Appointments

One good cover that's often used is a meeting with a therapist or counselor. Therapists can't reveal client names and seldom give any information out if called by outsiders. Make one visit first; then set one a month, but claim you have two. Always pay in cash. Use white out, photocopy the first receipt, and fill in dates on the copies as needed to leave lying around at home. Tell your therapist how important confidentiality is to you, especially regarding any inquiry from a spouse. Use the second appointment time each month to go play. Therapy was Mary's ploy, only hers was sex therapy as well as psychotherapy.

A Part-Time Job

Start a part-time job in door-to-door sales that are paid by commission: cosmetics, cleaning products, or any one of the "get rich quick schemes" that are available. This will work for a few weeks.

Gym Membership

Join a gym to work out a few times a week or some weight-loss program. Just don't be too successful at it and arouse suspicion. Keep complaining that you hate it, and it doesn't work.

Volunteer Work

Join a local volunteer organization or club, and then only show up occasionally enough to take home some anecdotes.

Enrichment Education

Start a night class at the local college, which you are prepared to fail, of course.

Exercise

Take up riding a bike in the cool evening hours. "Honey, you know how I need stress relief."

COVER YOUR ASS

THE AFFAIR IS underway. Mary didn't want to give up Joe or her husband. And she didn't want to be videotaped going down on her contractor. It goes without saying that unless you're stupid or want to be caught, you need to take precautions.

If there are two things that I could etch into your brain they would be: burn all paper traces—that includes the love poem—and do not meet in public. Sounds easy, doesn't it? Well, just when you are feeling everything is cool, it heats up to where hell might be a better spot for you than watching your expensive lawyer and ex-wife go after your assets. Your chances are greatly improved if you follow these basic ground rules for love on the sly.

Keep It Normal at Home

Attitude is critical for escaping detection. A suspicious spouse is sensitive to any alteration in your behavior. Even if you can't act worth a damn, you can avoid behaviors that are giveaways.

Don't Get Complacent

To conduct a successful double life, you must remain diligent. Too often, a client comes in paranoid that their spouse is in on the game. When I asked if their pattern has been changed, they confess grudgingly they have become sloppy about renting the same motel for an "early morning eye opener" or leaving receipts in desk drawers.

Don't Get Smug

There is no more threatening attitude when carrying on an extramarital affair than smugness. Just when you think you have the routine down and your better half is in the dark—knock, knock. A smug sheriff's deputy is serving you a document stating your children, home, and business are being ripped away from you.

Don't Court Danger

For some cheating spouses, the threat of exposure is as exciting as the sex. This is a dangerous game. The temptation to put the lover and the wife in the same room, to leave clues about, and to sabotage your own security might leave you without the lover, the bulk of your assets, the desired access to your children, and a wife to cheat on. If you're an excitement junkie, be careful that you don't end up in withdrawal because you pushed the envelope.

Don't Flaunt

If you have passive-aggressive tendencies or you're just plain pissed at your mate, you may find yourself dropping hints, such as claiming that "others" find you attractive. Don't show off your new figure since you've begun working out and losing weight.

Don't Use the Affair as a Weapon

You may begin arguing more or differently, claiming, you've "changed." Remarks designed to hurt the spouse or to communicate that you're not going to live with inattention, abuse, or disapproval anymore will raise a spouse's suspicions.

Get the Good Lawyer First

Just in case you do get caught, get the best divorce lawyer you can on your side first. Set up a consultation appointment, perhaps under the guise that you want some advice on the possibility of divorce, and what the ramifications might be. Once an attorney consults with you about the case, he shouldn't take your spouse's case if they come to him, if he has any ethical principles at all.

Behave Normally

Try to behave normally. Stay in character. Should you elect to step beyond your matrimonial confines, then there are several signs you must be aware of that can be dead giveaways that you are playing around. The following are some behavioral do's and don't's.

- Hide that you've begun a new exercise regimen.

- Disguise the fact that you're losing weight.

- Don't buy your spouse gifts without a reason.

- Don't suddenly begin to claim the need to work "overtime" or work late on a project.

- Don't let your spouse know you've bought a pager.

- Don't buy new underwear—or at least don't wear it at home. Mix it with the other underwear, or throw it in the laundry. Better yet, don't bring it in the house.

- Instruct your lover to never call your home.

- Don't alter your sexual patterns with your spouse.

- Don't dress differently; hide the sexy, smaller size, new threads you've been buying since you began the affair.

- Shower before coming home, but use unscented shampoo and make sure your hair is dry.

- Don't shave in the afternoon. The lover is going to have to live with razor burn.

- Don't come home smelling of alcohol or perfume.

- Don't alter your patterns with the family; if you've never done it before, don't miss a soccer game or a family dinner.

- Don't suddenly begin to leave for work early.

- Don't forget to put your wedding ring back on.

- Don't start spending more time on the computer.

- Repress your newly buoyant spirits and sudden and unexplained surge of energy.

- Destroy every incriminating scrap of paper; delete all phone and e-mail messages, and yes, toss the poem or card. That will make the next rule easier.

- Don't suddenly appear overly protective of your briefcase, calendar, and computer.

- Don't suddenly express new interest in eating different dishes.

- Resist the temptation to mention the lover's name to your wife.

HOW TO CONTACT YOUR LOVER WITHOUT DETECTION

THE TWO CARDINAL rules—keep no paper trail and never be seen in public—are obvious, but not always observed by the enthusiastic lover. If you're going to avoid detection you must:

- **Avoid any traceable link between you and the lover.**

- **Shake any private eye.**

- **Meet in a place no one knows about, changing venues often.**

- **Get no one—and I mean no one—else involved. You cannot mention the affair to anyone. Not colleagues or friends. This means you must resist the temptation to brag, vent, or share.**

I learned a lot from the cheating spouses I've tracked—what to do and what not to do. The spouse of one client was particularly crafty. We got him in the end, but he was good. One of the best I ever came up against. It took us quite a while to find out who the lover was. We started with the cell phone records. They were clean. We followed him, but he took U-turns and went down dead-end streets to see if he was being followed. We had to rent and switch vehicles. It was very expensive. It took three separate tail cars at once following him fifty miles.

Eventually, he made two of our cars and missed the first. With the third car, we watched as he pulled into a drive-through at McDonald's and circled to see if he was being followed. Then he parked his car, went in, and walked out with the chick. Leaving his car there, they went to a rented motel next to the fast food joint. Finally, we got our incriminating video footage. He was using all of the good evasive maneuvers.

He was smart. But not smart enough. It was a huge divorce. He lost millions of dollars. And all because he didn't make the third tail and then he let down his guard for a four-minute walk from McDonald's to the motel.

Put Nothing in Writing

I know it's tempting to write a love note or e-mail, but the cardinal rule of cheating is: Never put anything into writing and never send a card of any nature. Not one scrap of evidence in writing. This again and again comes back to haunt lovers in the courtroom. You can give your lover something other than a card for Valentine's Day, such as modeling that new lingerie. Anything your lover has from you should be able to be carried in the memory only. Some lovers even work out a private code in words or symbols to use between them.

Set Up a Contact Code or Story

Work out a cover name and cover story if your lover will be contacting you at work and then have the lover refrain from leaving a message for you. If they must, then make it something such as, "This is John with Liberty insurers and your policy will be here Monday at 1:00 p.m." To you it will really mean, "This is Toy Boy and the hot sex is on for 1:00 Monday at the usual place."

Don't Meet in Public

Never meet in public places. Eventually, you'll be seen by someone who knows one or both of you. You can easily be observed if you're being followed, and a cover story for why you're meeting outside of work or social gatherings will wear thin after one time.

But if you normally meet in social or business settings, act normally. Always, and I mean always, act professionally and business-like around your lover when anyone is in visual range. Never hold hands, hug, or pat them on the fanny. The cooler you act in public, the longer it will take for rumors to start circulating.

Make Untraceable Phone Contact

Use pay phones, a prepaid calling card, or a prepaid cell phone (not in your name). Make sure you use cash to pay for them. For prepaid cell phones, I like to use Virgin Mobile. You can use a false name when activating them and a false address. They are small in size and easily concealable. Set them to vibrate mode only and only you will know when it's ringing. These phones do have some interesting features. Delete all cell records in the phone data bank, and use *67 to block caller ID when dialing.

Never leave detailed messages in voice mail. Keep it short and use a coded message. And, set your voice mail to a default generic message. Do not record a message in your own voice.

While Joe was on the roof, Mary had lots of opportunity to plan their romps when she took him iced tea. Now that he was done with the roof, their contact had to be covert. I advised them to talk on prepaid cell phones that they'd taken out in a fake corporate name.

Make Untraceable E-mail Contact

Using the advice in Chapter 4, establish foolproof ways to evade detection by an electronic spy. And this means not your spouse, but the PI he or she hires to hack into your e-mail. Basically, you need to take the steps to protect your computer from invasion. That means using an anonymous browser, enabling password protection, using evidence-eliminator software, and deleting all e-mails and electronic history trails.

Practice Safe Sex

Planning ahead may take the spontaneity out of true love, but you owe it to your spouse, if not to yourself, to take the necessary precautions to reduce the possibility of STDs. Also, an unplanned pregnancy can really screw things up, so to speak.

Prepare a Lover's Kit to Cover Up

- Put tinted windows on your car. If you fool around in the car, tinted windows will defeat the video.

- Pack an extra set of clothes. Buy two exact sets of the same clothes. Keep one at another location or secure place just in case. You would not want to wear a shirt home reeking of a perfume that your wife does not use.

- Keep a pack of wet wipes handy. These remove odors of fresh shampoo or someone else's perfume.

- Carry a vial of the same brand perfume or aftershave used by you or your spouse. Moist towelettes are good for removing some perfume from your skin, but carrying a bottle of the same perfume or shaving lotion you normally use is even better, as it will mask your lover's brand and match what you should normally smell like.

- Use a broad-brimmed hat and sunglasses to help confuse ID photos.

- Carry work-related props in case you need a cover story. Take sales brochures, file folders, or something that seems work-related into the coffee shop or when entering an apartment, just in case. If you get caught with a lover, you need to have a good prop, or excuse for why you are there and with whom. Work all this out in advance and talk to your lover about how you will explain this meeting away in some believable manner if a friend, relative, colleague, or spouse happens upon you in Starbucks. The worst thing is to get caught and admit it, or stand there frustrated, not knowing what to say that sounds legit.

Damage Control If You Get Caught

You knew this might happen. You've been caught; now the question is, will your spouse let you repair this rift or will your mate push it to a divorce? The worst thing you can do is sit and wait, unprepared. Now, you have to read the rest of the book. You will have to conceal your whereabouts (Chapter 4), hide your assets (Chapter 6), and evade a tail (Chapter 8).

If your spouse has filed for divorce and claimed adultery, but there doesn't seem to be anything in writing, no video or photos, no proof of gifts, no phone records, no voice mail messages, and no other kind of solid evidence that could hold up in court, you may want to tough it out. You certainly don't want to get caught now. The jig is still up. Here are some tips for damage control. You can't completely cover your ass, but you don't have to show it more.

Never Admit to Having Sex

Unless your spouse walked in on you, no one can prove the act actually occurred. Yes, you held hands and had a flirtation. But adultery? Never. Even if your wife or husband says, "I have video footage," don't fold. Most video I shoot in the field simply shows hugging, kissing, or holding hands. If you're lucky and did not get caught going at it hot and heavy, you may be able to wiggle out with some excuse. That's up to you. But read my lips. Never, ever, admit to having sex. Period. If you used your head and did it behind closed doors, then chances are there is no hard evidence. On the other hand, if you did it in a public location—a car, a beach or a park bench—you may be toast. Otherwise, deny, point fingers, and make counter accusations! And, oh yeah, didn't you hear how they manipulate those digital pictures of the movie stars and put someone else's face on another person's body?

A point of interest: A strong magnet will erase a common video or audiotape. Just rub it back and forth on both sides of the cassette. A magnetic CB radio antenna works great. Just thought I'd pass that along.

Don't Contact the Lover

In the interest of saving your own ass, try not to contact the lover again. If things get truly serious, your spouse's lawyer will be serving the lover a subpoena anyway to ask embarrassing questions. If things get this deep, then you will need to talk to the lover and perhaps make sure the lover hires a separate attorney. You may have to contribute some cash for this. Just keep the communications down to "emergency reasons only."

Beware of the Lover

When one of the cheating bastards we nailed realized his goose was cooked, he tried to distance himself from the lover. She got pissed off and got together with the wife. The lover threatened to testify against him. He folded immediately and ended up without the lover, the wife, the condo in Belize, and the family mansion.

Find Out If Your Spouse Has Already Filed

You should have the best divorce lawyer already in reserve, as suggested earlier. (If you didn't, dig out a few dollars, contact the best lawyer, and meet with him to discuss your tactics and options in case your spouse does go overboard.) Then, try to find out if your spouse has already filed. Call all the best lawyers in the phone book and try to discuss your case with them. If you hit a lawyer that tells you your case is a conflict of interest, chances are your spouse has already spoken to them and is mustering the troops for an attack.

Corner the Legal Market

Because you have already talked to a big-gun lawyer or three as a part of covering your ass, they may very well turn your spouse down if he or she calls seeking a lawyer. At least this keeps your spouse from hiring the pit bull of the divorce business to come after your ass, and your spouse may have to settle for a less experienced lawyer.

Read Chapter 6: Protect Your Assets

It's critical to make all financial moves before any papers are filed. This is essential if you're going to recoup anything once your mate goes for the soft spot at the back of your neck. Empty joint accounts, convert everything to cash, move money offshore. This doesn't mean you don't share. You're just protecting your half.

Move to an Unknown Address

Read Chapter 4 and follow all the directions carefully for concealing your new home address as the divorce proceeds. Maybe you have to stay in town for the kids and work. But if you can leave town for a while, run, hide, and cover your ass somewhere nice.

Agree to Marriage Counseling

Chances are you didn't want a divorce. That's why you were having an affair and didn't leave your wife and kids. The marriage counselor can be your friend. Most marriage counselors will try to find an avenue to repair the damage if possible. Your making the suggestion to go to one also shows your spouse that you are remorseful for your awful conduct, you have the proper humility, and you are willing to grovel if that's what it takes. It's a hell of a lot cheaper than your $300-an-hour lawyer and splitting your life's assets into fragments.

Mary got away with her weekend, but she ultimately got caught when she left a poem from Joe (who couldn't write that well) in her underwear drawer. Her husband found it, and threatened divorce. She was distraught. She'd lost her mind over her roofer. She begged for marriage counseling, and ultimately she and her husband (who loved her very much) reconciled, and they're still married. She had a fling, got burned, and considers herself a lucky woman today. She still smiles when she thinks of Joe, however.

THREE

HOW TO PREPARE AN INTELLIGENCE FILE

YOUR ALREADY TWICE-DIVORCED daughter has just shocked you and sent your wife to bed with a Xanax by bringing home some yo-yo she claims is her fiancé. You want to find out where this cowboy has lived, if he has a criminal record, how many times he's been married, how many times he's been sued, if he's filed bankruptcy, if he's made secured loans, if he's ever had an alias, if he's got any professional licenses, if he's ever had a domestic-violence injunction, and if he's got a shaky driving record. Any of the facts in the intelligence report could be important information you might want to share with your easily manipulated middle child who unerringly picks losers. It's easier and cheaper than you think. Consider the following statistics:

- Number of sites online that will run an address history for as little as $25: over 200

- Cost to have a PI run a license tag: $30.00

- Cost for a private citizen to run a tag: a trip to the tag office and usually about $1.00 or less

- Cost of copying a seventy-eight-page divorce file in the county clerk's office: $78.00 plus about $5 for parking

- Average cost for a background check from an online service: from $100.00 to $300.00 depending on number of states involved and depth of the inquiry

- Typical number of years online public records go back: 7 years

- Typical time waiting in line at a public records office: at least 1 hour

- Cost in 1998 for me to run an intelligence file for a client: $1,000

- Cost in 2005 for me to run the same file: $100

Running an intelligence file is every investigator's first step, and it should be yours too. For 98 percent of the cases I work, I start by putting together an intelligence file on the target. This is the basic information I need whether I'm going to screen a potential son-in-law, tail a cheating spouse, conduct assets recovery on a crooked business partner, or trace a missing person. Assembling a profile entails everything from electronic detection, to the collection of data from a government office, to pretext work (that's a fancy term for skillful lying), to garbage confiscation (a.k.a. "dumpster diving").

Before you embark on the do-it-yourself PI work in Chapters 5 (assets recovery) and 7 (tailing a mark), you need to collect all relevant data on your target following the steps in this chapter. It doesn't matter if your ultimate goal is locating your favorite uncle Jack, finding your misplaced first husband to sign a document, conducting assets discovery on a sneaky relative, collecting evidence for a civil lawsuit, setting up surveillance on a cheating wife, or collecting evidence for a divorce, the first rule of investigation is to know your subject well, whether they're a misplaced friend or an adversary.

This is what I did for "Frank." He came to me looking for confirmation that his sister's new boyfriend, "Brett Bickle," was who he said he was. The guy seemed way too sneaky and insincere to Frank. Since Lulu had married and divorced two gigolos and, most recently, an outright thief, Frank was understandably hesitant when Lulu asked him to back her new squeeze in a boat-rental business. He was quite sure that Lulu's assessment—that her cowboy was business savvy and trustworthy—was not to be trusted. Did the little shit know anything about running a business? Had he once really run a boat-rental company in the islands? Because he felt sorry for his unlucky-in-love sister, Frank was willing to give Lulu's unemployed boyfriend a chance. But not without a background check first. He hired me to do the job, but you could do it yourself for just about nothing if you know where to look.

Most of what you need for your intelligence file comes from public records. Here, the federal laws governing public records are on your side. The rule of thumb is that if the entity holding the records (public utilities, voter registration, sheriff's department, police department, fire station, and/or tax assessor and collector) is funded by taxpayer dollars, you're entitled by law to have access to the records.

The electronic world has made initial data recovery a click away. While I'm going to assume nothing, I'm going to operate with the expectation that most people who attempt amateur PI work will have access to a computer, either at home, work, the library, or an Internet café. The key is knowing where to go to collect this information.

In many cases, you'll find all you need about your subject by perusing the public records available online. But beware. The information you get over the Internet may be incomplete. For a more thorough report, you'll need to go to the courthouse, city hall, tax assessor's office, and law enforcement stations in your community. Federal agencies, however, are impossible to crack without the help of a lawyer or PI.

Only you know how much of the necessary information you already have, but the steps outlined here will help you identify what's missing, what you need, and where and how to get it. To that end, I've included the steps, starting from zero. What you collect for your intelligence file, however, is completely dependent on how well you know the target (is it a spouse, the potential trophy wife of your aging dad, an employee you want to promote, or your mystery rival for a job or lover?) and your goals (fidelity surveillance, assets recovery, identity verification?).

To pull a public record off the Internet is free or cheap; copies of actual records at the courthouse usually cost a dollar a page. If you don't have access to a computer, don't worry. It's going to take longer with more effort, but it can all be done in person.

If you can make it to the courthouse, no interloper is safe from your scrutiny. Before Mom marries a stranger, you can hire yourself to legally and cheaply reassure your family that he's not pond scum in an expensive suit.

WHAT YOU NEED TO START AN INTELLIGENCE FILE

THIS COULD TAKE two minutes or two weeks, but without collecting the basics first, you could easily miss the key to your target's secret life. Your public records search (online and at the courthouse) could be woefully incomplete. To do a thorough intelligence file, you need some essential information that could open the door to other basic data and eventually hidden records. This is the information you will need to pretext the subject for credit card information, check out the subject's garbage for an offshore account, or access public records to see if your cheating asshole spouse bought an airplane with your life's savings. Hopefully, most or some of the basic data you already know:

- Full name (including middle name)

- Social security number (this is the key to everything else, but it's becoming more and more difficult to retrieve because of new laws and regulations designed to prevent identity theft)

- Date of birth

- Addresses

- Landline and cell phone numbers

- E-mail address

Most clients who come to me have at least one or more of these basics. Each one can be used to locate the remainder of the list. I actually have a menu which lists prices based on the starting piece of the puzzle. For example, if you have an address, you can get a name and phone number for $80; if you have the phone number, that can become all registered vehicles for $60; if you have the full name of your new boyfriend, I can access his ex-wife's name and address for $90.

The point is, one piece of the puzzle can open the door to everything else. Of course, a potential business partner, possible or current lover, and even a spouse may have hidden this information or lied about all or any of it. Discrepancies will surface soon enough. Locating alternate names, as well as illegal aliases—including legitimate maiden names, married names, and other forms of a legal name—is often a key step in the process. You may find out your current fiancé's criminal record when you look her up under her first married name.

I quickly discovered that "Brett Brickle" was an alias, which I had thought was an odd name. If Brett wanted to prey on gullible women, why didn't the idiot invent a name that had some sex appeal? The mystery deepened.

Useful Additional Information

Keep your eyes open for any of the following data; they're information that could lead to paydirt for anything from assets recovery to finding a missing tenant:

- Middle name or alias

- FEIN number of corporations, entities, or LLCs

- Current address of corporation or entity

- Maiden name

- Mother's maiden name

- All married names

- Favorite or current pet names

First, Get an Address

Even if you don't know the name of the bastard or bitch you're looking for, if you can get an address, you have a critical starting place to prepare the intelligence file, discover assets, or set up a surveillance.

As you will see in Chapter 6, the most important rule for hiding assets is hiding where you live. To hide your assets, you need to hide yourself. Thus, assets discovery, as well as surveillance, begins with locating the new home of the soon-to-be-ex spouse or business partner.

An estranged mate with a lawyer has very likely been advised to move to an unknown address. Unless the missing spouse has read Chapter 6 and taken extraordinary measures, you can find the new living place of the person birddogging you.

Conduct a Surveillance

If you have no name, no address, or no phone number, you may have to begin your intelligence file by shadowing the mark from a workplace or rendezvous spot until he or she enters an address and stays there for a length of time during which you can conduct a fixed surveillance, go through the garbage, or both. This means skipping ahead to Chapter 7. Determine the level of measures (such as disguising a car) you need to take, and follow the subject home.

Get the Address from a License Plate

The office where driver's license and car-registration records are kept is called different things and located in different places. It depends on the state. One state calls it the Tag Office; another state may call it the Tax Collector's Office and, in another, the name is the Department of Motor Vehicles. It could be in the county courthouse or located independently. There could be one office or branches. But, whatever it's called and wherever it is, you've got to find it. As a citizen, you can't get this critical information online.

RUNNING TAGS—If all you know is the license plate number for the Camry that seems to be following you or for the convertible that your lawyer husband's sexy client drives (the client he keeps meeting for lunch), you have the key to important public information.

To "run a tag," you give the clerk the license tag number and pay a nominal fee for the name of the person to whom the car is registered. This will usually include other information. When that tag prints out, you'll also get the driver's license number, date of birth, and address of the vehicle registrant. In addition, you may get bonus information: the official name (spelling, middle initial, full first name), a spouse's name, and, in some cases, the lien holder. If looking for assets, the lien holder is important, because there's a good chance the target has a checking and savings account at the same bank.

In all states, to run a tag you must comply with the Driver's Privacy Act, which is a federal law pertaining to driver's information. Your request must meet basic criteria and you may be required to sign a form under penalty of perjury during your request. It's important to note that in this brave new world, our privacy laws are changing daily, so please consult the laws of your own state before embarking on a records request. Additional laws may apply and differ from state to state. You can't just run a tag in every state. Some states also require a specific reason before they'll release the information. For example, you may need to claim that the car with that tag number hit you in an accident, or provide a similar legal need for the information.

When I ran the tag on Brett's Mustang, I discovered it was registered to Hilda Jones, who happened to have the same address as Brett's uncle, a condo where Brett was supposedly living.

Get the Address from the Water Company

While most utility companies won't reveal an address to go with a name or a name to go with an address, the water companies are very cooperative. They'll give you up on a dime. You don't need a pretext for the name. Simply say, "I'm trying to identify the customer at 111 Elm St." It works for me almost every time. But you may want to try a pretext if all you have is a name and you're looking for an address. Here's a sample question you can use:

> **YOU**: Hi, this is Janet with Smallville Public Utilities. We're trying to locate a previous customer who left owing us a balance. Do you have a hookup under Cynthia Smith?

Don't even try the electric company. Even a private eye can't get anywhere with them. The only people who can do it are information brokers. For $80, an information broker can take a name and turn it into an address. If I use one to break a phone number or an address, I triple the cost back to the client.

Get the Address from a Phone Number

If you have a telephone number from a bill, a caller ID, a note you found in your husband's pocket, a datebook, or any other source, you can get an address, and often the name of the caller.

On a visit to the house Frank had bought for Lulu after her third divorce, I asked him to check the caller ID on the landline. He also pulled numbers from Lulu's cell phone, which she always left lying around.

We knew Brett had a cell phone, but we were more interested in a repeated number on the caller ID of both of Lulu's phones that matched the prefixes for a local land line. Cell phone numbers can't easily be traced. Mr. Slick claimed that the condo he lived in belonged to his uncle, so there was no privacy. Thus, Lulu had only been there a few times, and she never told Frank the location. She and her new lover spent all of their time at Lulu's house.

Use a Reverse Telephone Directory

If you have the number, log onto the Internet and use a reverse telephone directory. Go to either www.google.com, www.411.com, or www.freeality.com/finde.htm. Type in the area code and number on the search line and press Enter. If the number is listed, the name and address of the owner of the telephone will appear. If it is a cell phone or nonpublished number, the screen will report "not found." If one of the sites above doesn't work, try them all.

Employ a Basic Pretext

If the information is "not found"—which means the target is using a cell phone or has an unpublished number—you have to go to the next step. Call the number and extract the name from the owner of the number by using a time-tested pretext or script. This is another way of saying you will need to lie. However, be warned that under the rules of the Federal Trade Commission, it's illegal to perform a pretext on any financial institution (private or public). The only legal option is to pre-text the subject or people who know the subject.

Before you make the call, you need to prepare. Block your identity either on your own phone by using *67, or by simply using a calling card. You may want to have a family member or friend make the call in case the person answering the phone turns out to be someone you know. You may also want to purchase a voice changer for $39.95 in case the person answering the phone turns out to be someone you know.

Next, practice what you're going to say. No pretext is completely trouble free, so you will want to be prepared for roadblocks. In the PI industry, we usually prepare for a pretext by role-playing with another agent who will throw up surprise questions. If you're uncomfortable doing a pretext yourself or your pretext fails, turn to a professional for help.

I suggest you try one of the following two scripts or pretexts, which are to be used when calling the subject. They are the Alaskan Operator Pretext or The Cell Phone Provider Pretext:

PRETEXT ONE: THE ALASKAN OPERATOR PRETEXT

MISS THING: Hello.

YOU: Hello, is this 555-666-7777? (the target number)

MISS THING: Yes, who is this?

YOU: This is Cynthia with Mountain Bell in Alaska. We're verifying that you made a call to Munich, Germany for $42.60 in the last thirty minutes.

MISS THING: Hell, no. I don't know anybody in Germany.

YOU: Ma'am, we suspected that was the case since we've had a cable cut here in Fairbanks. I'm showing your carrier there is Verizon. Is that correct?

MISS THING: Yes, that's my phone company, but I didn't make any damn call.

YOU: Ma'am, I'd like to apologize on behalf of Mountain Bell and we are going to issue an immediate credit to Verizon. I see here you're located in Florida?

MISS THING: Yeah, that's right.

YOU: Oh, you're so lucky. It's fifteen degrees below zero here. Okay. Just so we're sure this credit goes through, I'd like to send you a copy for your own records. Please give me the billing name and address there.

MISS THING: Yeah, this is Buffy LaRue at 14 Wilshire Court, Apt. B, Main St. Did you say 15 degrees below?

YOU: Yes, ma'am. Now, I'm going to include a courtesy card for $10 of free long-distance calling for the inconvenience.

MISS THING: Why, thank you.

YOU: Hang up. Now you got the bitch. Buffy LaRue? What kind of name is that? Buffy, your ass is mine.

Be prepared for surprises. When I called Brett's phone number planning to use the Alaskan pretext, I was surprised to discover Brett's "uncle" was a woman. It was probably this Hilda Jones, who had come up when I ran the license tag on Brett's Mustang.

Pretext Two: The Cell Phone Provider Pretext

- Identify the service provider (carrier).

- Login on Fonefinder.com and enter the phone number.

- Fonefinder will give you the carrier who has issued the number.

- An alternative is to call a common local carrier and ask if this is one of their numbers.

- Make a call to the cell phone and record their on-hold message.

- Call the number and be prepared with the following script:

YOU: Hello, is this 555-555-5555?

MISSING TENANT: Yes, who's this?

YOU: This is Gloria with Nextel Customer Service. We've had a problem with the assignment of your number.

MISSING TENANT: What do you mean?

YOU: As you are aware, recent regulations have allowed our customers to retain their old phone numbers no matter what cell company they choose. Your number has been inadvertently reassigned to an Alltel customer.

MISSING TENANT: What's this all about? I need my number. I've had this number for two years.

YOU: Yes, ma'am. That's why we're calling you. Of course, you can keep your number. I'm in repairs and I need to make out a new depac screen, making sure this number is reserved to you exclusively.

MISSING TENANT: What's a depac screen?

YOU: That's our in-house computer system, ma'am. Now I need to confirm the name and billing address for the account, please. And I assure you this will never happen again.

MISSING TENANT: I hope not. My name is . . .

If the Target Balks, Hit Her in the Wallet.
MISSING TENANT: Why do you need my name? Don't you have it?

YOU: I'm confirming your information so that I can assure you that this number stays in your name. I'm sorry. I'm trying to help, ma'am. The other account to which your number was assigned has already incurred $186 in calls, and we don't want billing to post this to your number. I'm trying to straighten this out, ma'am, and, unfortunately, if we don't solve this problem now, the number will be disconnected at 2:00 (make it approximately one hour away). I'm just trying to help.

If she refuses, say, "Thank you very much, ma'am," and hang up.

If You Have an Address, Get the Phone Number

If you already have the address from surveillance or the tag office or an Internet background search, you can use that information to access the target's phone numbers. The steps are the same ones used when you have the number, and want to get an address. Use Google, 411.com, or www.freeality.com/finde.htm and type in the address this time, instead of the phone number.

Trick the Subject

It's often possible to trick the subject into revealing his or her phone number by leaving a note on the door, under the door, or in the mail box. For this ploy, you will need a prepaid cell phone with caller ID, which you will leave for the subject. From caller ID, you can access the landline at that address.

THE MYSTERY NOTE—Tack a note to the door or place it in the mailbox using a phony name: "Please call me about a very private matter involving Cindy Smith (or Derrick Jones or Betsy Larson—make it up)." In my experience using this trick, curiosity overwhelms the subject and the mark makes the call. If you've got caller ID, you'll capture the landline or cell phone. Of course, if the target has their outgoing number blocked, this tactic won't work.

THE BUSINESS NOTE—Leave a note with a fake business card claiming to be with a new bank or some other entity just opening in town. "What would it take to get your business?" and/or "Call for a free gift."

Pretext People Who Know the Subject for the Address or Phone Number

Performing a pretext on a neighbor, relative, or coworker in person or by phone (depending on whether your first piece of the puzzle is the address or the phone number) is another effective method for gathering basic information, usually an address and/or phone number.

If you're going to perform the pretexts in person, you will want to apply the steps in Chapter 7 and adopt a disguise for your vehicle and yourself. Maybe your target has lived in town for only two years and you need to find out from which state to seek the public records. Sometimes, you can find a subject's previous address from neighbors with a simple phone call using a pretext. I frequently drive by, make sure the subject is not home, then either contact a neighbor directly or by phone and use a pretext to determine if the neighbor knows where the target lived before he or she moved here.

PRETEXT ONE: THE CLASSMATE PRETEXT

Claim that you are a former classmate who has just arrived in town, and you want to look up the subject: "I've been trying to reach Carrie, but I can never catch her at home. Do you have a number?"

PRETEXT TWO: THE AMERICAN INHERITANCE PRETEXT

YOU: My name is Bob Wilson with the American Inheritance Foundation. (It does not exist.)

SUBJECT'S SON: Inheritance? What's this about?

YOU: My research shows that you're related to (or, if it's not the subject's relative, substitute a neighbor of, colleague of, etc., as required) Fred Smith. I'm trying to close an old estate from 1919. The account is in excess of six figures and my information indicates that Fred could be an heir to this estate. Unfortunately, I don't have his address or phone number in order to contact him to verify this information. I was wondering if you could help me?

SUBJECT'S SON: What's the name on the estate?

YOU: The Smith family trust. I can't go into any other details until I verify that Fred's related to this estate. However, if this turns out to be true, he could be in line for a substantial sum.

SUBJECT'S SON: Well, I don't know . . .

YOU: (If the subject balks, give him a fake card with a prepaid cell phone number.) Here's my number and have him call me. And here's a PO box if Fred would prefer to write instead.

PRETEXT THREE: THE EMERGENCY PRETEXT

While the subject is away, approach the neighbors asking the phone number. Explain you're a relative, friend, or business associate, and you "need the number for emergencies." They may even give you the cell number. If the neighbor has seen you and/or the subject might recognize a description, you may find it prudent to disguise your car and/or wear a disguise.

DO A PUBLIC RECORDS SEARCH

THE NEXT STEP to building an intelligence file is to physically search for any public records that may exist on the subject. Remember, public-record law is on your side. The rule of thumb is that if the entity holding the records (public utilities, voter's registration, sheriff's department, police department, fire station, and/or tax assessor and collector) is funded by taxpayer dollars, you're entitled by law to have the record.

For a thorough intelligence file, you'll be accessing information from a variety of sources, first online and then, if more information is needed, from the physical files at a variety of locations. There are advantages to both methods. At the government offices you can see actual copies of entire files that include true images of each document. There are also some trade-offs.

The public records data online is much less complete than files accessed directly from the federal, state, country, and city offices. The information is often something like an index of what exists in the actual file or only pieces of the file that are available. If all you need is an ex-husband's name, you can easily pull this up online. If you want to know the reasons for the divorce, the witnesses at the hearing, and/or the terms of the divorce (such as alimony or child support judgments), you will have to make the trip to the courthouse.

And, sometimes, you may not have a choice. Based on changing laws, some files and some kinds of information are only available at the courthouse or city hall. But with the Internet, you can reach across distances to access files. You can pull a record from across the state or from out of Virginia or California without having to move from your desk chair. Many records are free if downloaded from the Internet, although most of the background-search services you use on the Internet charge a fee, usually less than $50, but this can still save you many hours of physical searching.

Once you've accessed the listing and case numbers for a file, either on your own computer at home (using some simple steps) or on a computer provided in every county office, you are ready to request the complete file from a clerk.

Begin the Search Online

Each site and/or government entity is housing different types of information, all of which may be relevant to your needs. In seconds, the computer can complete for you what used to cost thousands in fees and expenses to a private investigator.

Free Internet Search Engines

One simple first step—completely free—is to do what has become known as "googling" someone. You place your target's name in the search window of www.google.com or another major search engine and watch all sorts of information appear on the screen, from the genealogy your subject's aunt has done to any newspaper articles on your target. These articles could describe your subject's criminal arrests or convictions, involvement as a witness in a federal court case, receipt of awards, participation in a marathon, or application in a zoning variance hearing.

Use a variety of search engines. Each search engine could offer different information, so try them all. It's just a few clicks and could result in pay dirt: a middle name, a maiden name, a hometown, an arrest, a civil suit. These are the most common search engines used:

- www.google.com

- www.msn.com

- www.dogpile.com

- www.excite.com

- www.yahoo.com

- www.highbeam.com (focuses on media appearances)

If the subject doesn't come up, try the search engines again with variations. Use an alias, maiden name, or legal variations the subject might be using with their name. Type in their full name with the middle name, then try it with the middle initial, or by excluding it and see what happens.

You may not realize it, but after a time, files on the Internet are archived and will not show on search engines. So, if we are looking for older files back to or before 1996, we go to a site called the Wayback Machine: www.waybackmachine.org. This site will allow you to pull up old news articles and files on people from years past. These are records you probably won't discover when simply running a check through any of the free or commercial Internet search engines. It may hold gems on your mark you would not otherwise uncover. It is also free.

Next, go to www.crimetime.com/online.htm for some neat searches. Start at the top of the menu and go down each one. On this page, you can reverse phone numbers to address and name, trace an Internet email, do a death search, and more. All for free, of course.

Another great site for free is www.skipease.com. Here, you will find a vast list of searches that may turn up your subject. These include:

- **Reverse phone number**

- **Reverse address**

- **Nearby neighbor search**

- **Zip code locator**

- **Mail drop search**

- **Google university search**

- **Yahoo message posts**

- **Google message groups**

- **Craigslist message posts**

- **Pay phone locator**

- **AOLmember pages**

- **ICQ white pages**

- **Former coworkers and employee search**

And much, much more. All of them are free with the exception of the paid ads you will see by data firms. These ads are for paid services that will run advanced searches for your subject.

Finally, I recommend www.locateplus.com, which is a great phone database, however will cost a small fee.

When I did this initial search on Brett Bickle, I found nothing at all with that name. Since Brett had bragged to Frank about serving in the Gulf War and had been decorated, this should have definitely come up. I would soon find out that Brett Bickle didn't exist.

Government Online Links: Federal, State, and Local Public Records

If you begin with a search string for "free public records online," you will pull up about a dozen websites with links to government databases throughout the United States and often worldwide.

WWW.PUBLICRECORDFINDER.COM—This is one example of a website with links to government databases. One of these government websites is an excellent place to start. It's a free public records source directory that allows you to conduct a background search for any public records on your target throughout the United States. You can choose which records you want from a list of links that will take you to the particular database in a particular state or city.

Although free, the disadvantage of this service is that it only searches one state and municipality at a time. Unless you know the address history of your mark, you could easily miss the two years the rat spent married to someone in Mississippi before moving to Nebraska.

Although the social security number is always the key to the castle, often all you have and need is one small piece of the puzzle—a full name, a maiden name, a hometown address, a high school—to find the missing witness of your car-accident case. The computer screen will spill it all: state and federal records, including known addresses, civil judgments, criminal records, birth and death information, property and mortgage records, military records, marital history, etc.

Again, the information is limited, but may be enough to serve your needs. If you want to read detailed files, you can often access the case numbers and types of action (whether the target was sued or criminally charged) as well as other essential data to request the full records from a government office.

Frank was disgusted when I told him the truth about Bickle. Lulu's squeeze was what all of them were. Fakes and con men. She could pick losers with her eyes closed. No Brett Bickle showed up under military records, or under any records for that matter. That clearly wasn't his name.

WWW.FEDERALPACER.COM—As a rule of thumb, federal information is difficult to obtain without the help of a subpoena or private dick. But some is available. Pacer is an invaluable source if you believe that your target has had any dealings with Big Brother on the federal level— either civil or criminal. For a minimal fee, you can obtain case and docket information from the federal, appellate, district, and bankruptcy courts, as well as the U.S. Party/Case Index. You can request information about a particular individual or case. This service lists all parties and participants in a case, including judges, attorneys, trustees, and witnesses. Many courts offer imaged copies of documents.

Online Commercial Public Record Finders

These background check services are available throughout the Internet, usually for under $50, and are more complete than the free services provided by government agencies. However, you are provided raw data that are unanalyzed and incomplete. Still, you may quickly find what you need or gather the critical key—including case file numbers—to a more thorough search in person. The goal is to garner as much data as possible before you hit the streets and appear in person at the government offices.

One advantage of the commercial databases is that they are extremely efficient. They will search all fifty states at once, and records from anyplace your target has lived. (Using a government database requires you to check each state and locality separately.) If you think the person you're investigating could have lived somewhere you don't know, one of these services is an important resource that will cost considerably less than hiring me to run the same program. Armed with information about which states and cities your mark inhabited, you can then go back to the public record finder website and look him or her up by state.

Since I didn't have any idea where Brett was really from, I tried a commercial record finder. I soon hit paydirt. Brett's name and variations of it came up in Pascagoula, Mississippi; Miami, Florida; Taos, New Mexico; Rye, New York; and Sneads, Florida. From big cities to small towns. This guy got around.

I then went back to the free public record finder, clicked on Search the Fifty States, clicked on Florida, browsed several Florida databases, including the link, Inmates and Offenders, and entered Bickle and Brett. This link pulls up any person that's been incarcerated in a state correctional facility since 1992, along with charges, sentence, release date, aliases, and photograph. Bingo. There he was, big as life. Mr. Slick. His hair was shaved off, he was wearing prison blues, and his face was thin from prison food. But it was him. The little shit was trying to marry Lulu and had been convicted of grand theft, conspiracy to commit fraud, and abuse of the elderly. Abuse of the elderly? Could this be Hilda? Or his uncle? I also noted Brett's date of birth, which I would be needing as I continued running reports.

The bastard had lied to Lulu. He told her he was her age, which was forty-two, when in fact he was thirty-five. And his real name was Bernard Bonker. It would remain a mystery why he invented an equally unattractive name. When people create an alias, however, they often keep the first initials of their name. Brett (Bernard) also went by other names. The report listed aliases such as Candyman, Hooterboy, Bertram Ballister, Rhett Bickle, and Barry Brick. I then went back to each state and checked for each alias. Up came another forgery charge, this time in Wisconsin.

I then clicked back to the commercial database with Brett's aliases and discovered that the bastard had also lived in Chicago, Roundup,

Montana (population 1,000), and Marked Tree, Arkansas (population 1,500) under these different names. In Arkansas, he was charged with bank fraud and identity theft, and in Illinois, credit card fraud. In both cases, he'd fled across state lines while out on bail.

At this point, I also found out enough to nail Brett's (or Bernard's) ass to the floor. Brett's claim about winning the Medal of Honor in the Gulf War was phony, because while the troops were driving tanks through a sandstorm in Kuwait, Brett was cooling his heels in the Appalachee Correctional Institute in Sneads, Florida.

Accessing Public Records in Person

You may be conducting your entire public records investigation in person. If you have insurmountable tech anxiety or no access to the Internet, and don't want to involve anyone else, and thus are not going to do an electronic search, all of the information available in a click on the Internet can be collected in person if you have the patience, transportation, and time to visit a series of government offices.

Also, you may wish to expand your electronic search. A lot of information is, by law, not available on the Internet even though it is public record, so you will have no choice but to go to the courthouse or city hall to retrieve it. This is where the real gumshoe work begins. And, for a complete intelligence file, it's essential. It's your right to see the full file on any case, civil or criminal, and to see martial history and property transactions. You just have to show up in person to get it.

There is no one method to retrieve physical documents. Logically, every investigator—professional or amateur—must act on what pieces of the puzzle they have to start with. You can mix and match the order, but here's a typical route my operative or I might follow, regardless of the results of an initial electronic search. With the appropriate clerk at the courthouse, you'll find real estate, tax assessment rolls, lawsuits, and domestic injunctions. These records usually cost a dollar a page for anything you decide to copy. Next, visit the tax collector's office for verification of tax payments, vehicles, vessels, real estate, and all tangible property taxes. At the supervisor of elections, you can discover political affiliation and the address of residence (a source not to overlook). City hall will provide a business license, parking tickets, police calls, and booking photos. The collections department of county utilities can legally supply an updated address for your target.

Stop One: The License Tag Office

When I've finished collecting all the basics and am armed with all versions of the subject's name—all aliases, a corporate name that popped up, and different addresses—I usually begin the physical collection of evidence back at the tag office to run a tag and a tax roll to look for addresses under additional names.

Even though it's legally yours to have, some information can only be accessed in person at the tag office. Request the tax rolls by name or address. The printout has tax rolls going back ten years. These include: how much was paid in a given year, the address to which the bill was sent, the tax appraisal, and the name and address of the person who actually paid the taxes. Also available here are hunting and fishing licenses.

Stop Two: The County Courthouse

Once you've accessed the listing and case numbers for a file, either on your own computer at home (using the steps outlined above) or on the computers provided in every county office, all you need to do is request a file from the appropriate court clerk in the county courthouse to look up the following information.

CRIMINAL TRAFFIC OFFICE—In this office, you'll find driving history and traffic offenses. It's an invaluable resource that is also available online, either through public or commercial sources. Florida tried to sell driver's license photographs to public records databases in 2001, but the Florida Supreme Court struck it down. To take advantage of this resource, you need to take the subject's name, date of birth, and address to the county clerk's office and step over to window marked "criminal traffic." Ask the clerk to run a driver's history and license verification based on name and license number (or variations). This will give you several pieces of information. Look these documents over carefully.

Check to make sure that the registered owner on the tag matches the legal name on the license. Find previous driver's licenses, including those held in other states. If you're working under the idea that the legal name on the license was developed based on a birth certificate or driver's license from a previous state, confirm the validity of this theory. For example, if I'm looking for real estate, the previous address under which a driver held a license—which can be in another county—can provide a key.

Also, check when and where the first license was issued. Did the subject live there as long as he claimed and where he claimed? When we run this history, we also get a list of traffic tickets the subject has received in the past ten years under this driver's license and the location of where these tickets were issued. If your target is living in Florida, and you find five speeding tickets in another county north of you, the assumption is that the driver lived there at one time.

Check for different types of licenses. Does the driver hold a commercial license? This tells us to expand the search if the subject has a CDL (Commercial Driver's License). This is a prompt to look for tractors, trailers, and trucks that may be registered in other states. A trucking company might typically register in Nevada, so you know you have to look in Nevada if your target has a CDL.

If you have tickets issued to a vehicle registered to a corporation, you need to provide the clerk of courts with the ticket number and order a copy of the actual citation. The citation will include an address, a person's name, and the make and model of the vehicle the offender was driving. If a car is registered to a corporation, run the plates in Nevada. In Nevada, the plates are cheaper, the corporate tax is cheaper, and the cloak of privacy is often better.

I once discovered that the target I was profiling had a vintage 1960 Corvette that he was keeping in a warehouse. Unfortunately for him, he'd tested the speed limit when he snuck it out for a drive. We were able to add it to his assets in my client's divorce suit.

CRIMINAL RECORDS OFFICE—While still in the country courthouse, move next door to the criminal records office. One important question you'll be answering for your intelligence file is, "Does the subject have a criminal record?" Even if you've found arrests listed online, the only place you can get the complete file is at the criminal records office.

If you haven't acquired the arrest record and case numbers online, you can do it at the clerk's office. With the name and date of birth of the subject, conduct a criminal search at the computer in the clerk's office (click on criminal records instead of official records), where you will find a case number indicating a file for each arrest. If the person has had an arrest or a charge (even if dropped), each incident will have a case number leading to a file.

Once you have a case number, use the case number to request to inspect the file. The clerk will hand you the actual file, and you may sit down and examine each document. Make sure you bring a notepad and a handful of paperclips with you to take notes or mark each page you want to have copied. Bring cash to pay for copies. A file is typically fifty pages or longer, so the key sections you will want to read carefully and copy are:

- **Probable cause affidavit (usually three pages)**

- **Discovery list of all witnesses**

- **Final disposition of the case**

- **Still wanted (at large)**

- **Guilty**

- **Not guilty**

- Case dismissed

- No contest

Then, request copies of relevant page numbers, usually costing a dollar a page. In addition to the above, there is also other information usually available that you might find useful:

- Report (description of the incident)

- Investigating agency (police or sheriff)

- Sentence

- Name of subject's attorney

- Place incarcerated

- Restitution

- Names of witnesses

- Employers at time of the arrest, relatives, friends, or neighbors

- Judge who handled the case

- State's attorney who prosecuted the case

- Aliases and name variations used by the target. When examining the criminal file, you will see a list of any alias names or name variations that the subject has been known to use. These may include married names to made-up names to alternate identities.

- Place of birth (POB). One important thing you'll see is place of birth, sometimes marked. If this person was born in Memphis, he may have assets and property there. There's a good chance he spent a large portion of his life at the location.

- **Names and addresses of any victims.** If John Doe committed a battery or injury to a victim, it's important to get the victim's name because it's a good chance he or she may have already done half your assets work in an attempt to sue your mark for damages.

- **Possible accomplices with addresses.** These are a possible resource. All accomplices will know some history on your target.

- **Documents with "FBI" stamped on them.** This indicates an interstate offender. A reference to the FBI tells us that the target has arrest histories in other states. You can't get an FBI number unless you've violated in another state. Some jurisdictions will mark "interstate offender" or "multi-state offender." This is a prompt to run reports on the target in other states.

- **Address where the crime was committed.** This can be the key to a hitherto unknown current or previous address. Many criminal files will also list previous addresses in other counties in the state.

We hit pay dirt here. I discovered that Bernard had been sued by the family of Wayne Smith, accusing him of abusing the senior citizen. Seems Bernard, who was going by the alias of Barry Baxter (again, the BB initials), was hired as a caretaker for Wayne, doing odd jobs and lawn work, as well as shopping, driving him to doctor appointments, monitoring his medication, and all other jobs to assist Wayne. However, according to the complaint, Bernard left Wayne stranded on a park bench for four hours one day, and failed to give him his seizure medication, which resulted in an emergency-room visit. He also left him sitting for hours at a time unattended in front of a TV, using Wayne's car as his personal vehicle to go out for fun.

PULL CRIMINAL RECORDS FROM ANOTHER COUNTY OR STATE—If you have case numbers for criminal records from out of your home county, ask the criminal court clerk to mail you a copy of the file—or pertinent pages in the file—so you don't have to spend the time and money to travel to get it. A relaxed, polite approach works best.

> **YOU**: Ma'am, I'd like to order a copy of case number such and such. I'd like to know how many pages, so I know how much money to send.
>
> **CLERK**: We'll pull the file and call back. (When the clerk calls back with the file in front of him or her, the clerk will tell you the number of pages. It's not unusual for a file to reach fifty pages, and more is typical.)
>
> **YOU**: Thanks so much. I'm running on a budget, so would you be willing to send me the probability of cause affidavit, a discovery list of all witnesses, and the final disposition of the case?
>
> **CLERK**: Sure. That will be $3.25. What's the address? (You can pay by credit card.)
>
> **YOU**: (It's time for you to ask a crafty question.) In that file before you, does it show you the lawyer's name and phone number? He'll be interested in where Bernard's dog is.
>
> **CLERK**: Sure. Isn't it awful how the animals get left behind? (The clerk gives you the lawyer's name.)

The target's old attorney may be very willing to talk to you in exchange for information about his or her former client's whereabouts. There's a good chance the target failed to pay the lawyer all if not any of the defense costs. This is also an opportunity to be vindictive. You can engage in a little payback by telling the target's former lawyer where to find his sorry ass.

CLERK OF THE COURT (NONCRIMINAL RECORDS)—An extremely important source for an intelligence file are civil records. County offices have all noncriminal records and files going back ten years that are available on computers in the office and as more complete physical files. Information going back more than ten years is archived and must be requested in person from the clerk. It's stored on microfiche or in bound books. You do not have to provide a reason to request these files. They're public records.

Let's assume you have probably collected much of this basic general information online—marital history, property transactions, liens, mortgages, open-case civil lawsuits, etc.—but what's listed online is not complete. You, like Frank, will often want more data. Often it serves more accurately as an index to the actual files. The complete records must be accessed in person at the clerk's office, where a clerk at the counter will provide the files or direct you to the correct clerk or office or division.

If you give the county clerk of court any (or a combination of) name, address, birth date, and (if you have it) social security number, the clerk must give you copies of the files (usually in a folder), of all records relating to your subject. For the novice, I recommend walking up to every clerk at every station or counter and requesting information. The country clerk's office is actually a series of individual divisions, often each with its own office and clerk. Different divisions may have signs on the counter indicating different records—for example, marriage licenses or probate—but in smaller counties, all the information can be gathered from one clerk. Take a notepad and a handful of paperclips with you to take notes or mark each page you want to have copied. Bring cash to pay for copies. The main categories of civil records you'll find are:

Marriages: Every marriage license issued in a county is recorded indefinitely and is available either online, in the office computer, or—if older than ten years—in the archives. Since marriage license records are taken offline and archived after ten years, you will certainly want to continue marital history research here. Here you will learn if your subject was ever married in this county, when, and to whom.

By running a marital history on a guy in a fidelity case, I discovered that the sleazeball cheating on my client had another wife, not just a girlfriend. He'd been married in Massachusetts ten years earlier and had never gotten a divorce when he married my client. The dual marriages didn't void my client's marriage to the two-timer. She had to go through an annulment process. However, his "other wife," my client, took some satisfaction in turning him in, and they charged the cheating bastard with bigamy.

Divorce Records: All divorce files have a number, which you give to the clerk to request the file. The complete files will contain everything except the names of children, including:

- **Proceedings (summaries of hearings and trials)**

- **Witnesses at the hearing**

- **Settlements**

- **Custody decisions**

- **Child support actions**

- **Alimony**

- **Assets (including jewelry and collectables)**

- **Financial statements**

- **Addresses of ex-spouse**

- **Income information**

- **Business ownership**

- **Lawyer's name**

I was surprised when I first began my search that Bernard had never been married or divorced. The little shit was such a con man.

How did he miss out on the biggest con of all: a rich divorcée or widow? Lulu could not be the first woman Bernard took for a ride. Then I went back and checked the marriage and divorce records in the states where I had known previous addresses. Bam! This guy was unbelievable. Four marriages, none of which lasted longer than eight months. This lowlife scum had been sucking up to vulnerable women and successfully scamming them into marriage and settlements. The last wife was currently paying him alimony.

Property Transactions: Check the tax rolls, which go back ten years before they're archived. On these documents you'll find:

- **Name or names on deed (You may discover a co-owner or the name of a corporation or LLC you didn't know about.)**

- **Amount paid**

- **Assessment**

- **Address where notice was sent**

- **Person who paid the taxes (Sometimes the name and address of the person paying the taxes differs from the person who owns the property. I've uncovered love nests of more than one cheating husband by accessing tax rolls.)**

- **Current owners of the property**

- **Liens**

- **Mortgages (If you can get the name of a lien holder, this may provide you with the name of one of the banks or credit unions used by the subject from which you can ultimately seek bank account information for assets discovery, as covered in Chapter 5.)**

- **Deeds**

I go into much more detail on discovering property transactions in Chapter 5, page 159, if you need more information to help uncover hidden real estate assets.

Civil Court Cases: Within the clerk of court's office, there exist two levels for open and closed civil-court actions from which records can be retrieved; you need to request files from both jurisdictions. The first level is the circuit clerk of court, which deals with civil cases of more than $5,000. The second is the county clerk of court (aka small claims court) that handles civil cases under $5,000. This file, whether county or circuit court level, will be housed in a folder and may potentially contain any of the following documents:

- The summons. The summons alerts the defendant to the number of days he or she has to respond to an attached complaint.

- The complaint. The complaint tells you you're being sued and by whom. It lists the particulars of the lawsuit. For example, it might say, "on April 15, 2003, Joyce Smith ran over my prize azalea bushes and laughed about it. I've suffered mental anguish and am suing her for $3,000."

- The defense. The next page will contain any defense filed by the defendant. Joyce Smith responds, "I was swerving to avoid hitting the plaintiff's dog which was running loose. I couldn't stop. I'll see her in court."

- Notes on pretrial conferences and hearings. These are general descriptions of the proceedings written by lawyers or the parties themselves.

- Discovery lists of all witnesses. This lists all witnesses by name and address that either the defendant or plaintiff plan to call. Again, these can be useful contacts to talk to or pretext for more intelligence-file information.

- Trial proceedings. Here again is a summary of the actual trial proceedings written by the judge or court reporter. The actual transcript isn't in the file, but the name of the person who has the transcript is there. This document contains the court reporter's name.

- Court reporter's name. For an actual complete transcript of the trial, you can contact the court reporter and order a copy of the testimony. This is where you find the testimony of a neighbor who says Joyce did two lines of coke before she bopped the azalea bushes.

- Final judgment. Is the case open or closed and who got what if anything?

Probate Information: You can make copies of a will that's been probated. Probate information often reveals assets, who the personal representative is, relatives, who the family lawyer is, and certain debtors. While some of this may not be relevant now, it could be in the future.

Domestic Violence Injunctions: These records describe events of violence along with dates, witnesses, addresses, and locations of incidents. Sometimes, I have found a social security number in these files, an updated address, where the mark was served, and a date of birth. The petitions are generally public record and are obtained at a labeled counter in the clerk of court's office in the local courthouse.

Stop Three: Local Law Enforcement

At this point, you should have already looked up criminal and civil records at the courthouse. To look up any law enforcement activity involving your subject that does not involve an arrest or criminal activity, you must go to the local law departments. Local law enforcement records are not available online, but they are still public records to which you have a right. It's important to note that these records are destroyed after ten years. These records are generated and housed at three levels:

- County sheriff's department

- City police department

- State police department

Thus, noncriminal incident reports are available upon request at three separate locations for the county, city, and state levels. It's best to start with the county sheriff's department because the jails are run by the county. Even if a case is under city jurisdiction, the county will still have a record of the case because they control the jail.

SHERIFF'S DEPARTMENT—Ask directions to the records division. You may have to show ID and pass through metal detectors. There, you will request any and all records in their possession under your subject's name, date of birth, and address. As long as full name and date of birth match, they have to allow you to look at them. These records will include everything from your subject calling in a barking dog complaint to the domestic argument he had with his wife. These will be records that didn't result in an arrest, but the officer's collected information about the individual. Many times on these police reports, the departments will enter:

- Alias names

- Alternate addresses

- Unpublished phone numbers

- Angry neighbors

- Employers

- Girlfriends

- Family members

- Suspected drug use

- Booking photo

CITY AND STATE POLICE—Complete the same records check for arrest and nonarrest records at the local and state levels.

Stop Four: County Administration Offices

With a name and addresses you can access any records on your target connected to:

- Occupational licensing

- Building permits

- Code violations

- Environmental violations

- Animal control

Stop Five: Federal District Courthouse

A social security number would be most useful here. But, with the name, address, and birthday, you should be able to access files on your subject about bankruptcy, a federal criminal case, or federal civil lawsuits.

Stop Six: The Health Department

The health department is a statewide government office that houses the bureau of vital statistics for the state. Here you can collect some vital statistics about your target such as:

- Birth records that are not public record. However, you can get information on your own, but ID theft has kept these records off limits to the general public.

- Death records. These will list date, cause, and place of death.

- Health issues. Medical records are also off limits here, but you may find important little tidbits, such as dog bite

information. This could tell you the name of the mark's
dog, as well as to alert you to the fact that the mark
keeps four Rottweiler attack dogs, a handy thing to
know before knocking on the door.

Stop Seven: City Hall

You will be searching for the same types of information at the municipal level at city hall that you sought on the county level in the courthouse. Although there is some overlap and the types of records kept are the same, the data recorded differ from the county to city level. In addition to all the same types of information about civil matters available you found in the county, on the city level you'll be looking for city occupational permits, municipal tax records, and city police reports.

Stop Eight: The Department of Revenue

The state department of revenue office is also, in some states, referred to as the sales tax office (California calls it the Franchise Tax Board). You can't pull that up online. You must go to the state capitol or to a branch office, which is usually located in the major population center in your county. Here you can check to see if the mark has a permit to collect sales tax and you can often get a copy of his application. This will list lots of information regarding the target's business operations, the business location, the corporate FEIN number, the banking institution for the business, and even a checking account and bank location. If he or she has failed to pay the sales tax, you may even find a tax warrant for the mark in these files.

Stop Nine: The Supervisor of Elections

Maybe the sleazeball you're after didn't have the civic consciousness required to register to vote, but on the off chance that your target did, you can pick up an address at the office of the supervisor of elections. This is sometimes located in the courthouse, but it may be housed separately. Under the guise of checking out someone's political party affiliation, you can collect an address. Providing the name, you ask for a printout. Are they a registered voter? If so, what party and at what address? By law, you cannot write anything down. You can only inspect the printout, but not take any notes. You have to memorize the information.

Once I presented the file on Bernard, all Frank needed to do was decide what to do first. Should he tell Lulu, call the cops, or rat Bernard out to his former lawyers and wives?

FOUR

PROTECT YOUR IDENTITY AND PRIVACY

THERE ARE MANY reasons why it's in your best interest to maintain your privacy and protect your identity. Knowledge is power, and you don't want to willingly give power over yourself to anyone. It's empowering to give out only that information about yourself that you choose to, especially when you know someone like me can crack your personal history like an egg if you haven't taken preventive measures. Consider these statistics:

- The number of official state, federal, and local government databases collecting information on each American: Thousands

- How accessible your personal information is to an adversary in public official records: 100 percent

- Number of Americans who have been victims of identity theft in 2004: 9.9 million

- Number of states with laws to control identity theft: 50

- Number of aliases one person can have: Unlimited

- Number of laws against holding an alias: 0

- Level of difficulty (1 to 10, 10 highest) to legally change your name: 1

- Number of states that make driving records available to the public: 38

- Number of stalking cases for 2003: 1,006,974

- Number of files the United States government has on its citizens: 3.5 billion and counting

When you're pulled over and the cop runs your tag, he also learns your current address, date of birth, social security number, whether or not you have a concealed weapons permit, whether you have any outstanding warrants, and even the last time the police had contact with you—along with your picture. If a flatfoot pulls any of my tags, they find the name of a corporation. Because there's no driver's license required for a corporate car, the cop has no photograph of me to match with a name, and no way to access my concealed weapons permit, my PI license, or even my name. I always tell a cop who I am, but it's my choice.

And it's your choice. There's absolutely nothing illegal about protecting your privacy and making it difficult for your snooping neighbors or government officials to get the goods on you. In fact, with identity theft as the new designer crime, keeping your personal life secret is good business. Or, like me, you may just want to protect yourself from unwelcome visitors. I don't want any irate wives or husbands I've busted finding my home address from my vehicle registration, showing up at 3:00 a.m, and tapping on my front door with an ax. You don't have to be avoiding the IRS, your ex-spouse, or the FBI—there are plenty of other reasons for protecting your identity as much as possible.

As I mentioned in the last chapter, I begin every case by building an intelligence file. By the time I actually knock on the door or put a mark under surveillance, I know the mark's date of birth, real hair color, eye color, and the color car he or she drives. I will know the spouse's name and all known relatives, as well as the mortgage company for the house, the mark's criminal arrest history, and the speeding ticket he or she got last weekend. Pulling a file oftentimes lets me know if a mark's interests lie in fishing, hunting, golf, business, or porn. I will also know the value of the home and the unpublished home phone number, and where the mark has lived for the last fifteen years. Incidentally, my file will also contain the neighbors that lived next door to him in all those locations and their current phone numbers. I will know every corporation he or she owns and every fictitious business they've ever started. In many cases, I can also identify his current cell phone number in case a pretext call becomes necessary during the investigation. In many cases, I even know a lot about income based on court files such as divorce cases, financial affidavits, and financing statements.

I have no intention of using any of this information, other than in the interest of my client. However, as you can see from the last chapter, anyone with an Internet connection can find the same information, and that person may have other ideas on how to use it. They might use it to buy cars, apply for loans and credit cards, or even frame you for a crime. In this chapter, I'm going to show you some of the ways you can conceal and layer your private information in such a way that it will require intense effort for snoops to gain meaningful and accurate information about you. Often, the point is to discourage and frustrate the efforts of an amateur or pro trying to spy on your personal habits. The more successfully you can fade and disappear from public records, the most successful you will be hiding your assets (Chapter 6), avoiding surveillance (Chapter 8), and operating undetected in cyberspace (below).

THREADING

THERE IS ONE concept you must understand in order to protect your privacy from prying eyes, and that is the significance of one small piece of information and how it's tied to your life. I call this process "threading." Threading is the process that enables a computer system to lock onto a single piece of information and then develop each and every thread that contains that phrase, address, or name.

Let's assume that you would like to set up a trust, which you wish to remain a secret, but you're going to need a mailing address for documents and mail. If you use your home address, the name of that trust and entity will show up when I run your address on the Internet. If you subscribe to a magazine in the name of that trust, it will be revealed to me because the magazine is being sent to your home address.

On the other hand, if I didn't know the name of the trust or that it was associated with you, it would be impossible for me to identify it as an asset owned or identified with you. This same system of threading is used with such information as your vehicle ownership, fishing license, corporate ownership, real estate ownership, recreational vehicles, and all facets of your life. There are thousands of companies in business that spend each hour of each working day doing nothing but assembling information on each of us.

I learned many of my personal privacy protection techniques early in my career when I tried and failed to find a drug kingpin who had set up my client as a patsy in a drug trafficking case. All my client knew about the big criminal behind the operation was his boss's false name and the address of the farm where drug deals went down. The drug boss had created a bulletproof layer of privacy by purchasing a farm (where the crop was marijuana, guarded by men with submachine guns) under a bogus name, complete with magazine subscriptions and junk mail, then registering his vehicle to a corporation that was a front, and cutting all paper trails to his actual identity. It was all very legal, and very effective. I never found him. But you can use the same methods, legally, if you want to fade from sight.

To do this, you need to disappear from the public records. While you can't cover old records—they already exist—from this day forward, you can make it difficult for people to find your information. For example, you can remove yourself right now from public records if you build a new mailing address, use prepaid cell phones, pay bills with money orders, have your real mail sent to an untraceable locale, use an untraceable landline phone in your home, and conceal your identity as the person using television cable service, garbage pickup, or any public utility.

Most of the clients who ask for this service are trying to avoid process servers, creditors, a prying ex-spouse, government tax authorities, snooping government officials, a predatory gigolo or gold-digger, a blackmailer, criminals trying to steal your identity and/or your car, business competitors, prying employers, ex-partners, nosy neighbors, and annoying relatives.

That's what "George Burton" wanted after he went through a ball-breaking, gut-twisting, heart-stopping divorce. His ex-wife had cheated on him with her coworker; however when George retaliated with a spite fuck, his ex, the cheating bitch, cleaned his clock in court. She won a large settlement because she had more legal evidence on him than he had on her. In fact, he had nothing on her. He only knew what she'd done; he had no proof, or at least nothing that would impress a judge. His wife had hired a private eye, and during the divorce proceedings, he was shocked at all the information that her lawyer had assembled on him: the name of his mistress, how many times he visited her, and the types of lingerie and perfume he bought his girlfriend and his wife. (The mistress got the better of that exchange, which didn't help George at all.)

When the last document was signed, George vowed that no one would ever be able to discover the details of his personal life again. How much money he made, how he spent it, where he lived, and what he drove were nobody's business. Besides, he had an ex-girlfriend and an ex-wife looking for his ass now, both of whom had private investigators.

I told George to follow the same steps I've outlined in this chapter, the same steps you can use to remove yourself from the public records as quickly and as thoroughly as possible. You can't actually conceal your identity, but you can make it so difficult to find out anything about you that many adversaries and investigators will give up. Methodically and deliberately, you can cut off all the trails to your private information from the likes of me.

PROTECT YOUR PRIVACY IN CYBERSPACE

IT'S NOT ACTUALLY accurate to talk about privacy in cyberspace. There isn't any. The FBI searches e-mails for key words these days without a court order. I'm assuming you have a virus protection program, but that won't protect you from Uncle Sam. The future is even more bleak, as recently the government has come up with a "Trojan horse" program and the major manufacturers of security programs have agreed not to install blocking programs in their antivirus programs and firewalls. In other words, the government can and may read anything you send on the Internet. However, there are some things you can do to become a hard target for common snoopers and to even secure certain files.

Here is a very informative site about privacy tools, antimonitoring software, Trojans, and advice for newcomers to privacy protection: www.anti-keyloggers.com/antimonitoring_products.html

Eliminate Spyware on Your Hard Drive

One way you leave yourself open to identity theft and intrusion in cyberspace is from spyware programs, Trojan horses, cookies, and data miners, which are all on your hard drive spying on you and your lifestyle. They are also taking up space and using up memory. To preserve your privacy, you need to eliminate them. They are inserted in your computer either from a website or through software you load. Have you ever wondered how companies get your information to send you spam and actually know your first name? There was a data miner inserted into your computer by a website. This slows your computer down because it's collecting data and it eats up your memory. When you eliminate these spies, your computer works better.

And it's a growing problem. Many of the programs you're buying off the store shelf can also include these privacy invasion tools right from the manufacturer, so the manufacturer can track your buying patterns and websites you visit, all in the name of efficient marketing. It's time to get rid of these spies recording every detail of your cyber lifestyle. It's time to disable these puppies.

Adware

Fortunately for us, this has become such a widespread problem that some companies are promoting this free software that you can download to eliminate these privacy-invading software programs. It removes them from your hard drive. My favorite program for this is made by a company named Lavasoft (www.lavasoft.com). It's totally free and the name of the program is Adware. It's simple to install and user-friendly, and don't be surprised the first time you run it if you find that you've been the victim of dozens of spies.

Trojan Horses

These are programs designed by hackers and deposited without your permission on your computer; these files can be embedded in photographs or any file you download; they are used to steal passwords, steal identity, and to infect your hard drive with viruses. Protect yourself by using a software program called Spybot and/or a virus program.

Cookies

These are small programs that a website deposits on your computer without your knowledge, usually used to determine how many times you visited their site; they take up space and are used for marketing and monitoring. You can protect yourself by using a software like Norton's Systemworks or a free program such as Cookie Crusher. You can also open up your web browser, go to the Preferences section under the file menu, and select Cookies. You can then delete the ones on your hard drive, and usually set preferences on how you want your computer to treat cookies. You can deny downloading them, for instance.

Data Miner

These cyberspy programs are normally used by companies for marketing and to monitor your activity on the Internet. They enter your hard drive from free downloads, websites, and purchased software. Protect yourself: Use Ad-Aware.

Protect Your Data from Other People

You may want to protect your personal data and Internet activity from anyone who has access to your computer—a parent, spouse, sibling, roommate, or coworker, or a PI hired by one of these.

Stop Spies at Boot Up

- **Install a Fingerprint Security System. This is a scanner that attaches to your computer, and allows only you to access your computer based on your fingerprint match to a prerecorded image of your fingerprint.**

- **Set a Secret Administrative Password. If you put in a secret password, the computer refuses to boot up unless the user knows the password. This can be done through your computer's operating software. For Windows, go to the BIOS screen (Press F3 or F8 for the basic settings for your computer). Click on set administrative password. Enter a secret password that only you will know.**

Switch Internet Access to a Network

For further security, go to the server you use to access the Internet and set the parameters to look for a network connection when you're not using the computer. The network connection doesn't exist on your home computer. Unable to find the network connection, the server won't open. When you're ready to go on the net, switch back to modem dial up.

Protect Your E-mail

If you don't want the recipient of an e-mail to trace you, these are sites to which you can send an e-mail that will repackage it, using an untraceable e-mail address and send it on. Most are free, so the price is right, including:

- www.angelfire.com/ct/cizauskas/anony.html

- www.virtualdrawing.com/fakemail/mixmaster.autistici.org/cgi-bin/mixemail-user.cgi

- www.the-cloak.com/anonymous-surfing-home.html

Use an Encryption Program

The best program going is an encryption program called PGP, which stands for Pretty Good Privacy and was made by Phil Zimmerman. This program can encrypt a file that would take years for several super computers to break into. It's free and easy to use. You can download it at web.mit.edu/network/pgp.html.

Shred Your Files

Just as with your garbage, your Internet trash needs to be shredded. When you simply hit the delete key, all it does is basically place your files in the garbage can (recycle bin) or hide it in your basement (hard drive cache).

However, there are several free programs that will "shred" those files and make them nearly impossible to recover or read. The program works just like a shredder, but takes time to process the file. You simply drag and drop the file to the shredder program and tell it how much to overwrite and destroy the evidence. You can use a standard wipe or, if it is really a hot file, use the Government Wipe function, which is the same one most government agencies use to destroy electronic tracks. Free file shredders can be found at www.tucows.com/preview/266328.html and http://mutilatefilewiper.com.

Surf the Web without Detection

Many eyes are watching which websites you visit. If someone close to home or with access to your computer might want to spy on your private lifestyle choices, buying patterns, or personal recreation, you can either stop the trail before you visit a site or eliminate your activity when you shut down for the night.

Use Anonymizer

This is a program that will lay a wall between you and those tracking your surfing on the Internet. The sites are www.anonymization.com and www.megaproxy.com.

Use Evidence Eliminator

The program called Evidence Eliminator automatically removes web trails, cookies, and cached files (files which you deleted but the hard drive retained). You run it manually once a day just before you shut off your computer or before you go to work and leave your computer unattended.

CHANGE YOUR NAME

BY CHANGING YOUR name completely or using a variety of variations on your name, you can frustrate and confuse any pursuer, professional or amateur, looking for your address, your assets, and your credit card number. Using name variations to disguise your identity is also extra insurance against identity theft.

Adopt an Alias

It's a radical step, but it's completely legal and often the appropriate choice. Perhaps you want to cut ties with relatives you fear or despise; perhaps you want to deter scrutiny from things in your past of which you are no longer proud, even criminal records. Hey, you were sixteen when that happened. You don't do that anymore. My clients have also changed their names to avoid a stalker or a dangerous ex-spouse. Witnesses in criminal or civil proceedings who don't necessarily qualify or desire the radical option of the witness protection program often change their names.

A name change is an effective step for fading from public records and evading an amateur or professional detective from snooping on your private life—as long as there has been no court action yet. Timing is everything. If you haven't been served a legal document, this is as easy as going to the local clerk of court's office at the county court house, picking up the blank forms, filling them out, and turning them back to the clerk of court. A short hearing—which is only a formality—is set before a judge in the judge's chambers. The judge will look at the form and ask if you're changing your name for fraudulent purposes, to dodge creditors or to avoid a legal proceeding. Basically, the judge wants to know if you're trying to shirk a responsibility or currently involved in a legal proceeding and trying to evade being served. If you answer "no" to these questions and satisfy the judge that you have no criminal intent, the judge will stamp his approval on the paperwork and you can go home a completely different person.

Use Different Versions of Your Real Name

On official documents, including trusts, tax rolls, loans, and your driver's license, confuse pursuers with different versions of your name. If the investigator doesn't have your social security number, he or she will easily miss some assets and other official information.

When creating an entity, applying for a loan or license, or filling out any official form, present alternate versions of your name. For example, although you'll find a place for it on any form you fill out, there is no law that says you have to use a middle initial. If your name is John Frederick Jones and if the pursuer is running a search based on your name, leaving out the middle initial will place you in the category with a thousand other Joneses in the United States. You can also alter the presentation of your name: Johnny Jones, J. Frederick Jones, J. F. Jones, Freddy Jones, etc. This can confuse the hell out of anyone, even those with lots of investigative firepower.

PROTECT YOUR SOCIAL SECURITY NUMBER

YOUR SOCIAL SECURITY number is key to every private element in your life, and thus the investigator's most useful piece of data. Your social security is also the linchpin for identity and credit card theft.

This is the piece of information you want to protect, but most citizens give it up readily, even when they don't have to. It's requested on financial applications, medical forms, and employment files. Of course, it's the policy of a bank, an insurance company, or an employer to refuse to conduct business with you without it. So, you have to spill it if you want the loan, the credit card, or the job. But you don't have to give it to your doctor, the utility company, the telephone company, or, in fact, any entity requesting it.

Imagine "Maggie," a secretary in a doctor's office who is trying to support a drug habit and a house full of fellow druggies, stealing patients' social security numbers and ordering a dozen credit cards in their name to share with her dealer. Cases like this are happening every day all over the country, and the number keeps rising.

Stonewalling
One way to keep yourself off public records is to refuse to reveal your social security number indiscriminately. Refuse to put it on everything

except the financial, government, and employment applications that are integral to your life, or on forms for which it is legally required. For example, there is no law requiring you to supply your number on:

- **Medical forms**

- **Utility company applications**

- **Casual labor (under $400)**

- **Police reports**

- **Firearm applications**

When purchasing a firearm, the form always asks for a social security number to run the required background check. However, in reading the law, you will see that this is optional. They will never tell you that at the local gun shop and often look shocked when you reply, "No, I don't give my number out, and it's not required by law."

You'll be amazed at how many institutions and organizations are requesting that number when they have no legal standing to do so. You can refuse to provide your social security number unless the entity requesting it can show you a specific law where it's required. Ironically, there are no federal laws that say anyone must obtain a social security number. However, there are many laws that will not allow you to do something unless you have one.

In the state of Texas, there was a lawsuit because employers insisted on having social security numbers for their employees. A sixteen-year-old applied and was hired by Taco Bell. When he filled out an application, he left the line of his social security number blank. After a week or two, the manager discovered this and requested the number. The young man refused. As a result, he was terminated and sent home. The young man's father was a local attorney who sued Taco Bell claiming there was no law that required his son to provide this information to an employer.

The attorney won the case and, as a result, Taco Bell has deleted the section asking for the number from the application. However, the employer can ask for a social security number for a W-2 form. If you don't fill out the W-2 form, at the end of the year, you face a $50 fine. Most employers would not indulge this because they think what's become a matter of practice is the law. It's not.

The point is to be aware and selective. Although legally you can refuse to provide your social security to a bank, they will deny you an account or loan without it. It's their policy, and allowed under the current laws. If you need the job, the loan, the credit card, and the insurance, then give them the number, but don't just indiscriminately give it up when you don't have to.

Tweaking

One method some people have used to frustrate those spying on them in public records is to tweak their social security number. Now, you would be crossing the legal line if you used a false social security number to commit a crime, such as fraudulently filling out a loan application. But I've seen many people tweak their numbers and none has ever been charged with using a false social security number. We all know that some numbers are transposed by accident. If the bank or a police report asks for a social security number, the applicant may write it down one digit off. The most frequently transposed numbers are 3 and 5 and 9 and 4. If your 9 is picked up as a 4, that's not your fault. That's how you write your nines. A year down the road, it will be your word against the clerk who's no longer employed there about who made the mistake.

Another case where you're asked for your social security number is your doctor's office. It's not illegal to tweak a number on a form if the entity has no lawful right to demand it in the first place. If they insist on a number, then you make one up or tweak yours. This would also apply at a hospital, utility company, or for casual labor under $400.

You may want to transpose the last digit to prevent snooping office personnel from prying further into your life. You don't want them to run a credit report. And you don't want them to give the number to an investigator. Tweaking may frustrate and confuse your pursuers.

CONCEAL YOUR ADDRESS

CONCEALING WHERE YOU live is the key to protecting your privacy. To hide yourself and your assets, you must conceal your actual address, one of the critical threads to all things about you. If no one knows where you live, no angry boyfriend, PI, or do-it-yourself dick can put you under surveillance. You don't want the bill for a secret storage-rental facility, bank statements from the Caymans, or credit card information coming to a known address. This is as good as putting them online. In neon.

Move Immediately

To legally "hide out" at a new address, you must do it before any legal action has occurred—before you've been served with divorce papers or any other court order. Once law enforcement has served you papers at a particular address, you're stuck keeping your lease. It's a violation to move.

On the other hand, if you move to an unknown address before there's a court order, you haven't violated any laws. If process servers can't find you, they can't serve you with papers. Until they serve you, the court has no jurisdiction. By hiding your location, you make all of this more difficult and buy time. The more difficult you make it, the more expensive it is and eventually your adversary could cut his or her losses and drop the charges or the pursuit.

Having learned this lesson, George was ready. After following the steps in this chapter, he rented a nondescript apartment to which no mail, no deliverymen, no relatives, no process servers, and no angry enemies would ever come. The whole world was pissed off at him, but he could kick back with a gritty novel and relax. No one knew where he lived. His only friend—one drunken high school buddy—met him at the donut shop or bar and didn't have a clue where he lived.

Cut Off the Paper Trail to Your Address

You may be physically hidden, but you still need to have a way to receive utility, tax, and credit card bills; bank statements; and any other necessary legal correspondence. Once you're in a hidden apartment—or, even if it's too late and your ex and their pack of attorneys know where you live—the very next step is to create a new mailing address or addresses with which you've never been associated. You need to break any paper trails that could lead to this new address. I learned this lesson working that drug case I mentioned in the beginning of this chapter. It was one of the methods the drug dealer used to elude me. He purchased 160 acres of land, used an attorney to handle the closing, and the property had a thirty-foot mobile home on it. He established a false identity and had magazine subscriptions mailed to that name and address, so all his drug business was conducted under an assumed name and address. He also got mail under an alias name. Thus, any "colleagues" who wanted to turn state's evidence didn't have his real identity.

But you aren't, hopefully, on the run trying to evade capture—you merely want to protect your privacy—and maybe your safety. When it comes time to register a car or boat, or apply for any license you have, even if it's in your name, you need to register to some address other than your own. The following steps are perfectly legal and can mean the difference between being safe and sound and being found.

A Simple Address Switch

Concealing your actual address could be as simple as having your mail sent to an alternative address: the home or post office box of a relative or trusted friend.

"IN CARE OF" A FRIEND OR RELATIVE—This is the most obvious and cheapest option. However, you run the risks involved of including someone else in your private matters and the possibility that your ex has given the names of all your relatives and friends to her pit bull of a lawyer.

UNITED STATES POST OFFICE BOX—Today you are required to show picture ID and sign an "I swear" form to secure a driver's license. Thus, whatever address you choose to list on your driver's license will be the one that authorities give out to process servers and people trying to locate you. What's on your driver's license? Is it a post office box? It's up to you to declare where your actual residence is. Many people have multiple addresses. A lot of them have a physical address, yet choose to list a PO box on their vehicle registration, credit apps, or driver's license.

COMMERCIAL POST OFFICE BOX—Here, we're talking about Mailboxes, Etc. or the new UPS stores. Sometimes, this is a better choice than the United States Postal Service, because the privately owned concerns don't have as many rules and restrictions and can sometimes better preserve your identity.

Establish a Decoy Address

One of the best ways to frustrate investigators is to purchase a wooden post and a rural mailbox and establish a fake address as a decoy. Drive outside the city and down a dirt road until you find an intersection with a long row of rural mailboxes. The longer the better. An area where houses are being built, bought, and sold is best. This address becomes the one that shows up online when an investigator runs a report. It will lead the searchers away from your real address in town where you live and get your real mail.

- Look at the sequence of numbers and set your box at the end of the line. Write your real name on the side of the mailbox.

- While sitting in your real address in town, start filling out junk mail coupons with this rural address as the return address and sending off for things such as life insurance offers and record clubs. Once you're on a few mailing lists, the box will start to fill up.

- Pick up your rural mail once a week or less on different days and times. That will make the carrier less suspicious than if you establish a weekend pattern, suggesting this is a second home.

- Use great care in collecting your mail and always be on the lookout for a surveillance unit.

- If an investigator like me were to pull a file on you, this address would show up. Your pursuers will think you live there and that a house exists. Since the area is rural, they'll search their asses off for the house and not find it. Eventually, they'll give up, as they cannot afford major man hours day after day watching the mailbox and driving country roads.

- If by some chance a process server should get this address, we want him to sit out there for days on end waiting for you to pick up your mail or search the miles of rural countryside looking for your house that doesn't exist.

George was hot on this option. At a local hardware store, he purchased a rural mailbox and post. He then drove into the countryside along the dirt and gravel roads until he located an intersection with a row of approximately fifteen mailboxes. Because everyone lived in back-country lanes, there were no houses near the boxes. At three o'clock in the morning on a Saturday, he pulled out his posthole diggers and went to work. On Monday morning, the local postal carrier was making his routine deliveries when he noticed a new resident had

had moved in on Hilldale Lane. The bright new mailbox in sixteenth position displayed the next consecutive mailbox number and George's name.

Then, as George parked himself in front of *Days of Our Lives* on the tube, he subscribed to some free publications under this name and sent out inquiries for life insurance flyers and other mass mailing requests. George got himself on as many mailing lists as possible. In short order, George's mailbox was just as active as his neighbors' and filled with typical junk mail, which established in the postman's mind that George Burton lived on Hilldale Lane. No investigators or process servers were able to find or serve George there, of course. He was sitting comfortably thirty-five miles away in his untraceable apartment.

Create an Alias at a Secret Address

At the address listed above, you had mail you didn't want, like junk mail, sent to that location to add one layer of security. But you still need an address to receive mail you do want, like legal documents. You can rent a United States or commercial post office box under the name of an untraceable trust (see below) and have your mail sent there.

Follow the same steps as for setting up a fake rural address (above), but put a name not your own on the mailbox, and then have mail to you delivered in care of the fake name.

George found a third country lane and painted the name "Betsy Berry" on the new mailbox, his new alias and/or the name of his female alter ego. To this mailbox, he had mail delivered as "George Burton c/o Betsy Berry." This is where he received official mail from his attorney, trust documents, and financial statements.

Tweak Your Official Address

CHANGE OFFICIAL ADDRESSES ON LICENSES AND REGISTRA-TIONS—Register your car, boat, or plane at one of the above alternative addresses. We prefer a PO box number on your driver's license. They may ask for a physical address on the application, but you live where you say you live. That's always subject to change.

CHANGE YOUR ADDRESS ON THE TAX ROLLS—If you own property, you're on a tax roll, and every year the county will mail taxes to whatever address you provide them. You may want to change your tax notice and have it mailed to your rural mailbox or some other location in the future to preserve your private residential address.

Create an Entity that Is Difficult to Trace

The creation of a trust, a Limited Liability Corporation (LLC), or a limited partnership to which mail can be sent is another layer in your privacy armor, another way to frustrate those trying to find your real address.

A trust created in the states of Nevada or Delaware offers more secrecy due to the liberal laws in those states. You don't have to be a citizen of those states to take advantage of their privacy laws. For example, you can create a trust and name it something generic such as "Security Family Trust" by contacting an attorney in Nevada or Delaware who can set up the trust and do all of the paperwork. The only name an investigator will find on the trust is that of the registered agent—in this case, your lawyer. You and your lawyer have confidentiality. No such trust is recorded in your home state and Nevada won't release this information. At the same time, the name "Nevada" appears nowhere on the trust documents. It's a dead end. There is more on creating trusts in Chapter 6.

Picture the average citizen being stopped by the police. The first thing the officer does is call his tag into central dispatch for an identity on vehicle ownership. Normally, a driver's license number, photo, address, gun permit, social security number, and all kinds of other information will come up. But if the car is registered to a trust or corporation, the only thing that comes up on his screen is the vehicle info, not the human information: the name of the trust and the PO box. The officer doesn't have date of birth, criminal history, and/or social security number. You don't want an officer coming to your car with predisposed attitude because you had a shoplifting charge at eighteen. The bottom line is that you don't want anyone having your private home address, not even a police officer.

George had this lesson well learned in a short time. He established a trust named Family Security Trust, and put the title to his new car in the name of a trust c/o Betsy at his second rural mailbox. The closest an investigator pulling a tag can come to finding out where George lived is nada. Anyone who runs the tag will find only the name and address of the trust with no connection to George. His ex and her lawyer may be suspicious of this (hell, George's ex watched him riding around in an expensive sports car for months), but they can't prove that George bought and owns the car because it is registered to Family Security Trust.

Furthermore, George rented an apartment in the name of the trust and put his water bill, electric, and phone in the name of the trust. He insulated his privacy further by placing the trust in the name of his cousin.

It's important to recall at this point that no trusts are bulletproof, but it will be very difficult to prove George's ownership of a vehicle or attach that money.

ESTABLISH TELEPHONE PRIVACY

AS OUTLINED IN Chapters 1 and 3, investigators and snoops often breach telephone company security and obtain a list of your associates by getting a record of all your incoming and outgoing local calls and/or a copy of the phone bill. They can also use it to find your address. There are steps you can take to help thwart this.

Cell Phone

Normal cell phone records are easily located through good investigative techniques like those outlined in Chapters 1 and 3. But prepaid cell phones and cell phones taken out in an untraceable name provide the ultimate protection from scrutiny. Be sure to have the bills sent to a bogus address. Never use a credit card to buy more time on a prepaid phone. Always use cash.

Land Line

The next problem you will have is your land line telephone. It's a good idea to have a nonpublished phone number and a better idea to have your home telephone listed in a totally different name or to use a prepaid service.

You can list the phone in the name of someone you know. Choose a relative or friend who trusts you enough to have the phone placed in their name. Or, you can list the phone in the name of an invented roommate or child. Many people wishing to protect their privacy make up a name and claim that it's their teenage son or roommate and have the phone actually listed in any name of their choosing. The phone company doesn't know their children, their names, or how many you have. Once the teenager phone is set up, go ahead and cancel the main line that was in your listed name.

USE A PREPAID LANDLINE SERVICE—Reconex (800-275-8223) provides local telephone service to people who have been denied service, or do not wish to purchase service from their Regional Bell Operating Company (RBOC). This service is provided on a prepaid basis, so there are no deposit requirements or credit checks. Since Reconex is a reseller of local telephone service, it leases telephone lines from your local telephone company and resells them to you on a prepaid basis. This eliminates the need for deposits, credit checks, ID, and social security questions.

ESTABLISH DUAL-STATE CITIZENSHIP

ONE WAY TO frustrate someone trying to find your address is to establish dual-state citizenship through your driver's license and car registration.

Driver's License

It's legal to live in one state and hold a driver's license from another as long as you maintain an address in the state listed on your license. While you can't have licenses from two different states in your possession at the same time, many citizens who maintain a second address in another state elect to be licensed in the state with the strictest privacy laws, no matter how they distribute their time between the two states. Some people hold a New York driver's license (New York offering more privacy protection than most states) in order to add an extra layer of secrecy while they reside in Florida. If all records point to New York, there's a good chance anyone researching you will miss your home in Florida.

To further frustrate those looking for you, open a PO box in Florida with the New York address. You have to show ID to rent a box; your license has the New York address and that's what appears in the postal records. A process server has the authority to request postal records. However, if the only address of record for the box is based on a New York driver's license, that's what the server walks away with. You may live a block from the post office, but they'll never know it.

Out-of-State Car Registration

There are many advantages to registering vehicles in other states. Not just financial, but privacy benefits as well. In the United States, thirty-eight states currently make driving information available to the public. The remainder of those states have laws in place to prevent private information in your driver's license and car registration file from being released to the public, including driving history, age, address, and vehicle information.

FILE DIVORCE ELSEWHERE

ANOTHER WAY AN investigator can find out about you is through the divorce information filed in the clerk of court's office. As you can see by looking at this section in Chapter 3, a wealth of information about you is freely available to any nosy yo-yo who asks in the public records. You may want to hide the divorce or just the financial statements associated with the divorce. Either way, this painful business was once your business, and you'd like to keep it that way.

There are two good, reasonably priced options to obtain a legal divorce that are recognized in all fifty states and yet protect this information from snooping: file in another county in your state or get an out-of-state divorce online.

Out of County
It's legal to file all the divorce proceedings in another county in your state. This is much cheaper than the extra charges connected with sealing the records in your home county. If you do all the paperwork and are filing one county over, you have only incurred some travel charges, but thoroughly frustrated anyone looking up information about you through divorce records.

Out-of-State Online
The Las Vegas and Reno divorce sites (www.nevadadivorce.com) are legendary. Most people know that the one location in the United States where you can obtain an out-of-state divorce without being a resident of that state is Nevada. But now you can do the deed over the Internet. For $900, you can have a divorce that's complete and legal in fifty states without having to appear in court or leave your living room.

The divorce must be noncontested and not involve any property or custody settlement issues. All of that needs to be ironed out at home. Now, when someone starts looking for your assets through this source, they can't find it. It's all out on some hard drive file in Nevada.

Out-of-Country Online

You can also file over the Internet (www.legalservicesproviders.com/no-residency-divorce.htm) in the lesser known locales of Guam and the Dominican Republic. They are both United States territories, and there are no residency requirements in either country in order to obtain a divorce. The divorce from both of these nations is recognized by all fifty states. The cost begins at $875, requires no separation requirement, and takes about four to five weeks for completion. Both parties must consent. Several legal firms offer this service over the Internet, and by filling out the forms online and using a credit card, you are five weeks out from being single.

George's divorce was definitely contested, so he didn't have this option. His wife would rather stick an ice pick in her own foot than give him a chance to avoid the public humiliation she had planned for him.

VOLUNTEER NOTHING

FORMS AND POLICIES can be misleading. Much of the information requested on the applications and forms by financial institutions, medical offices, and government entities is not legally mandatory. Although the form asks for it, you don't have to provide your social security number to a doctor or your occupation to the government (as stated above). Much of the information you give out about yourself you're actually volunteering. Many people just accept that the requestor has a lawful right for the information simply because the question appears on the form. Your response should be, "show me the law."

Read the law and understand exactly what the statute requires before filling out any of these forms. You'll be surprised.

Often, we are "trained" to blindly follow the herd mentality, so as a result, millions of people give away their privacy daily without question. Question everything, especially when it comes to the government.

Refuse to Give the Location of Your Birth

You do not ever have to legally give this information to anyone except when applying for a passport. Many of the forms you fill out may ask for location of birth, however. Refuse. The reason law enforcement and financial institutions ask is because should anyone start to look for you and you've decided to skip town, it's a good bet the city where you were born still has family members who know where you are, or, that you have returned to your hometown. Your family knows other things about you that a skilled private eye might extract with a clever pretext. This is one of the most important mistakes skips make. They don't cut all ties with the past. They run to where they have some kind of support.

Refuse to Give Your Occupation

Every application requests this, but in most cases, you don't legally have to supply it. For example, a section on the application for renewal for a concealed weapons permit asks for "occupation." Under the statute, "occupation" is not a requirement for the renewal. I always leave it blank, but I estimate that 99 percent of all applicants have blindly answered this question. Some government snoop had decided to insert that question in the form and, if you answer it, the whole world will know what you do for a living because you volunteered it.

Think Before You Sign

Anytime someone requests you to fill out a form requiring a signature, that implies the information is voluntary, not mandatory. If it were mandatory, your signature wouldn't be required. If someone is asking for your signature, you have a choice to comply or not. Technically, you can refuse to supply the information and refuse to sign.

In addition, if you sign a document, you are in effect agreeing to something or entering into a sort of contract. I often see this happen with patients at a walk-in medical clinic. Even though they intend to pay cash for the visit, they sign the required form without reading the small print. They just signed a form allowing the doctor to release their medical information, holding the doctor harmless for treatment in some cases, and agreeing to attorney's fees and costs on any collection action. In fact, without legally having to, people sign such a release when paying cash and have no insurance carrier. Why?

It's your right to ask, "Is it mandatory? What if I don't sign?" You should always question those things. For what have you given consent? What will the information be used for? You will be amazed at how many clerks and government employees will stutter and stammer if you ask to see the law they are relying upon. This usually involves requesting their supervisor, who many times will admit there is no such law.

Marketers are using contests to get people's okay to be added to a call list (small print) because you signed a consent form unknown to you. You give permission to be on a mailing list if you enter an e-mail address. They're going to sell your name to 1,000 other call lists. By entering the contest, you've consented.

Your signature is not mandatory on a driver's license or on the application either, although you'd be refused a driver's license, legally. There is no law requiring it, so technically, you can refuse to sign it. On a driver's license, the signature is granting consent to sobriety tests, drug screening, mandatory insurance laws, and consenting to abide by a certain set of rules.

CREATE SHORT-TERM ALTERNATE IDENTITIES

HERE ARE SOME ways to create a short-term alternate identity that may be helpful. But, you need to understand it must be used for superficial reasons, not official reasons. You make up a name that you want to use for two or three weeks and discard. This is only illegal if you use the identity for an illegal purpose. For a month, you can be Larry Jones with an insurance card, a professional identity card, credit cards, and a clergy ID in your wallet. You might even fool a pro going through your decoy wallet.

Free Registrations

Make up a name to fill out any free forms for free information, especially insurance offers for life or health insurance and credit cards. Shortly after mailing these out, you'll start to receive junk mail in the new alias. Some of it will contain worthless plastic cards with the name. For example, Veteran's Life Insurance sends you a card with an eagle and your new name. This is your temporary insurance card.

Unactivated Credit Cards

Save those credit cards you receive but don't activate under your new name. All plastic cards look semi-official. If I look through your wallet, I might believe you're Larry Jones or that I have the wrong person.

Professional Identity Kits

Besides plastic cards, there is an NIC police supply source on the Internet that sells identity card kits. One example is the American Press Association (www.nic-inc.com). They'll send you a neat ID kit where you type in your name, a space to insert your photograph, address, and other personal information, and plastic laminate, where you can iron the laminate together to make it appear an official press card. This adds one more piece to the alias you're building and identifies you as a reporter. If you don't want to be a reporter, NIC sells approximately twenty other identity cards for other occupations that look very professional and semi-official. All this will help you further your new identity.

Become a Priest

Some sites on the Internet will provide you with a complete clergy kit. When is the last time you challenged a preacher about his identity?

Universal Life Church (www.ulcseminary.org) has a form you can fill out, and the church will ordain you as a minister and send you a free certificate announcing your new appointment with whatever name you provide. Of course, you'll also get some advertising for things like blank marriage and baptismal forms. You can use these with your new congregation for a week or two. You can also get a sign so you can park in a clergy parking space in an airport or hospital. They have collars for sale, too, if you wish to adopt a disguise.

Become a Professional Something

You may opt for one of the many education certificates sold on the net attesting to your past accomplishments (suitable for framing of course) with your alias on it. This will include identity cards that can go in your decoy wallet.

In George's case, he didn't need to become a priest to mask his identity. By following the advice I had given him, he had successfully buried himself beneath layers of secrecy, removed himself from public records, and lived a quiet and secret life. Through a few simple moves, George made his world private and secure. He continued to use prepaid cellphones, register his cars in trusts in other states, and use untraceable cash and traveler's checks. His ex could no longer harass him because she didn't know his phone numbers or where he lived. No more keyed cars, no more calls to his employer, and best of all, no more screeching voice on his phone every weekend.

FIVE

HOW TO DISCOVER HIDDEN ASSETS

PERHAPS YOU THINK your business partner, sneaky sister, or deceased father's trophy wife with the ridiculously enhanced breasts has been hiding cash that is supposed to be shared with you. You know that your father had lots of investments, ones that his child bride is now responsible for as executrix of the estate. She's telling you, however, that these funds were depleted for medical expenses and you know that's impossible. You suspect she's emptied the accounts and parked the bucks in offshore accounts and big-ticket luxury items, like big, expensive yachts. The gold-digger loved boats. If you don't find the money by settlement day, you could be losing thousands of dollars that your father wanted you to have. Her chances of keeping the money are pretty good, considering the following statistics:

- **Estimated amount of private money hidden in offshore accounts: $5 trillion**

- Limit on number of legal aliases a person can have: 0

- Number of safe deposit boxes a person can legally hold: Unlimited

- Number of bank accounts a person can legally open: Unlimited

- Percentage of single older women living alone who are legally poor: 20

- Percentage income change of divorced women: −73

- Percentage income change of divorced men: +43

- Average cost of hiring a private eye to conduct assets discovery: $1,200 to $4,000

- Typical cost for you to find the hidden assets yourself: $0 to $325

Following the paper trail (public and private records) requires only the time and knowledge of where to access public records for boats, vehicles, real estate, corporations, secured loans, divorce settlements, and inheritance information. All of these are avenues to the money that your deceased dad's trophy wife is now controlling. A few bucks to photocopy these records could represent thousands of dollars in your attorney's hands and in a court of law.

Over the years, about 10 percent of my clients have come to me for assets-discovery work like that described above. They are from all walks of life and are usually in some kind of legal contest: divorce, a civil lawsuit, or an estate settlement. I've been asked to do assets recovery on a sneaky spouse, a cheating business partner, or a prospective business deal that's just too good to be true. I've found money for inheritors looking for hidden cash, creditors seeking a deadbeat's hidden stash, landlords looking for the assets of a prospective tenant or one who's bolted, spouses looking for unpaid alimony and child support, plaintiffs seeking unpaid judgments, and lawyers trying to establish a potential client's assets.

One local lawyer, "Lawyer James," called because he was considering taking on a case for a client who had been injured in an accident and wanted to sue the other driver. Before Lawyer James took the case, however, he wanted to know if it was worth his time as he would be working it on a contingent fee basis. James was willing to spend a little cash for me to find out that the other driver was in bankruptcy and had very few assets. Lawyer James didn't take the case and saved himself hours of free labor.

Of the 10 percent of my clientele who hire me to find the hidden assets (usually involving a will), the majority could do much of the legwork themselves. Although it's nearly impossible to find all of the assets most of the time—for example, if the target goes alone deep in the woods and buries the damn money and tells no one—I will give you the steps to find, and hopefully recover, what you believe is rightfully yours. A person with minimal financial resources, but a lot of motivation, can conduct the same search for which I charge thousands of dollars.

Like the family of "Roberta Johnson," who were desperate to locate the assets of their vulnerable, widowed mother. She had married her ballroom dancing instructor, Hans, a child groom who turned out to be a swarmy gigolo and opportunist.

Originally, Roberta told her kids that she'd kept her assets separate from her new boy toy. She was in her late 70s when she was swept off her feet on the dance floor by Hans, who claimed he was in his mid-fifties. But Roberta's family had never seen the prenuptial agreement. And they'd seen little of Roberta since they couldn't stand the creep who had bamboozled her.

They came to me after Roberta called the family together to say that Hans was no prince. She told them she was ashamed to admit it, but she had put Hans on her checking account and there was $100,000 missing. So was Hans.

When the kids questioned whether the prenuptial agreement would protect her, she told them the next piece of bad news: "I never insisted on having him sign it." As the money had begun to evaporate, Roberta believed he was investing it in his ballroom dancing–software business. On further investigation, however, her oldest son had discovered that Hans had no clients. He had no business. And the actual amount of missing money was closer to half a million dollars.

Now, Roberta was close to broke, and the children wanted back money they considered to be their inheritance when the time came. They weren't going to let Hans walk off with it. They were also scrambling to cover Mom's mortgage, so they were motivated to find the missing half a million bucks. They hired me to help them, but mostly, they helped themselves with the advice I gave them, and saved themselves a bunch of money. You can, too.

An important skill that needs to be mastered is the art of pretext we've employed in earlier chapters. This chapter will, for example, give you the script to call the target with a bogus credit-card inquiry that should uncover otherwise hidden financial information. I'll share pretext work that is legal. One professional, who my firm used for years to locate offshore accounts, made as much as $20,000 a week simply from pretext work. He's doing time now for crossing the line. The feds didn't appreciate his expertise. In this chapter, I'll reveal the secrets of impersonating a credit card company or an inheritance finder to pretext the gold-digger herself to get essential financial information without crossing that line.

But not all the work this chapter outlines is so clean. If you know that the selfish bastard you're divorcing had a large hoard of cash hidden somewhere on the property, you need to get a shovel. Possession is the law. If you find it, it becomes yours. He's got to prove it's his. You also may have to roll up your sleeves and engage in the art of dumpster diving. Of course, if you have the cash to hire me to do that, you can forgo buying the rubber gloves.

One note of explanation. You can't actually *recover* stolen assets (except with a shovel in the yard). For assets recovery, you'll need to work with your lawyer, who will take the role normally played by a PI. Much of what we do and what I'm showing you how to do in this chapter is assets "discovery." Where are the missing assets? You're compiling a list of entities, people, and institutions that your attorney will subpoena for proof of concealed goods. Then, they can be subpoenaed with regard to those missing assets. You're collecting the name of the target's bank, landlord, girlfriend, ex-business partner, and estranged employer. You're getting the addresses of the mark's clients, which can be matched against income on the tax returns. Bank account numbers, credit card statements, receipts, and storage facility invoices taken from the target's garbage behind the office—this is the information your attorney needs to seek a legal judgment against the person who snatched the assets to help you legally regain what's yours. Armed with the right information, it's up to your lawyer to clean out the scoundrel in court.

If you're a quick study, you can collect the critical information by following a paper trail, accessing public records, and/or engaging in a pretext. Instead of paying me $4,000 to look for the missing money with no guarantee I could find it, Roberta's family could have followed the steps in this chapter. You can too.

GRAB THE LOOT YOURSELF

IF IT'S STILL possible, empty the joint accounts yourself and hide the valuables. Possession really is nine-tenths of the law. If you've got it, there's a good chance you can keep it. While you're fighting to get back the $100,000 your unscrupulous partner took from the joint account, he or she's depleting every dime of that money hiring a lawyer to fight you. I've seen it happen a hundred times—if the bastard has already beat you to it. You may want to go on the offensive and employ the techniques of Chapter 6 to store the disputed marital money or joint business assets.

It was too late for Roberta. Her half a million was gone. But what did Hans do with it? She and her kids were motivated to find the money and the bastard who took it.

IS IT TOO LATE? DO YOU NEED THE PROS?

THIS IS WAR. At this point, it may be too late to take the basic steps outlined in this chapter. If you find clear indicators that your target guessed you were going to bail, and that he or she has hired the professionals, disappeared to an unknown address, and dumped all the assets you shared into a foreign country, you may need to hire a PI to track down the yacht harbored in Nice. And then, recovery is going to be long and difficult.

When a mark goes undercover with the goods, an amateur's chances for recovery are much slimmer. If your target has pulled a preemptive move or knows you're looking and already skipped out of your radar, your spouse, lover, business partner, or sister may be using any of the techniques outlined in the next chapter. Read Chapter 6 and determine if your mark has already taken steps to stash the cash and other assets.

How a PI Can Help

If the scum you found cheating has skipped town and the process servers can't find him or her, or you can't find the new address using the techniques in Chapter 3, give in and hire a private investigator.

Also, all of the assets you're trying to find may be secure in a trust you can't trace, as discussed in Chapter 4. Since the smart trustee has registered his or her trust in a name that is not associated with your target, the only way you can break a trust is find a name in the mark's garbage and have your lawyer subpoena the records. If you believe there's a trust, this is a good time to hire a PI.

You will also need to hire a PI to conduct assets discovery if the money or assets could be hidden offshore or in a foreign country like Guernsey or Dubai.

How You Can Help Your PI

If you're still in contact with or living with the slimeball who you realize is secretly pilfering your joint assets, play it cool. Remember, possession is the goal. Don't tip off the subject with unusual questions, accusations, implied suspicions, threats, or sloppy detective work (return the checkbook to the same place in the drawer).

Don't ask an estranged husband if he owns an airplane you don't know about. Don't ask a wife you're about to divorce if she's got a secret bank account. They won't tell you the answer. Instead, you're warning them to open an offshore account, hire a lawyer, and buy this book.

Prepare Your Own Intelligence Report

Apply the lessons of Chapter 3 and assemble as much information as possible about the person who has the money. Gather what you can easily collect for free before you pay the professionals. There is still a wealth of information about your target in public records that will help your PI find the guy who skipped town, and a list of people and places to subpoena that you can gather on your nickel instead of your lawyer's.

Even if the target has made you and disappeared with everything, you can still do some of the footwork before you spend the bucks on a PI. Boot up the computer or put on your shades and a wig for early morning fixed surveillance. You may find a hidden bank account, your target's current address, or your baseball card collection which the target tried to sell on eBay.

Roberta and her children figured Hans was too dumb (Roberta had been taken in by his dyed blonde hair, not his brain), greedy, and arrogant to evade assets discovery. They assembled their own intelligence file, collecting as much as possible for the PI who would complete the European end of the search (Hans is Swiss, after all) and the lawyer who would serve the subpoenas on the entities, credit card companies, and financial institutions uncovered by Roberta's kids.

GATHER THE BASIC DATA FOR A HIDDEN-ASSETS SEARCH

SO YOUR SMUG spouse, thieving business partner, or brother with a gambling habit have no idea that you're checking out their assets. The following are the steps you'll want to take in the most logical order for your case, leaving out steps that aren't relevant.

Before you can recover what Daddy's new wife Buffy hid from you and your siblings, you need to know what to look for, prove that it exists, where it's hidden, and what it's worth. You might know that she did it, but you need proof that the cash Buffy got from selling your father's coin collection still exists. She can smile at a judge, readjust her bosoms, and admit she blew it at the track. It's up to you to discover if it's hidden in the backyard or reinvested in secret holdings.

Let's see what key information you already know about that bitch Buffy, your rotten-to-the-bone ex-partner, or the sleaze who took your sister to the cleaners. And let's see what you still need to find out to conduct a successful campaign of assets recovery. These are the preparatory steps.

Gather Basic Information

Hopefully, if someone knew you well enough to access your assets and abscond with them, you already have the following basic information in your file. However, if you're not married to, living with, or related to the person you're pursuing, you may need to take the extra steps to assemble the basic information. Furthermore, a potential business partner, potential or current lover, and even a spouse may have lied about all of these basic things:

- Full name (including middle name)

- Current address

- All phone numbers

- Social security number

- E-mail address(es)

- Mother's maiden name

- Place of birth

- Favorite pet name

- Business addresses and phone numbers

- Webpage address

- FEIN number of corporations, entities, or LLCs

- Current address of corporation or entity

Find the Address

Assets discovery often begins with locating the new home of the estranged spouse or business partner. A subject's home address is critical to an assets search. As you would learn from reading Chapters 3 and 6, the first thing a successful thief does is conceal his or her address. Chapter 6 advises your adversary to hide themselves to hide their assets.

It wasn't just Roberta's money that was missing. Hans was, too. An estranged mate with a lawyer has very likely been advised to move to an unknown address. Unless the missing spouse has read Chapter 6 and taken extraordinary measures, you can find the new living place of the person bird-dogging you.

If you know where they work or hang out, review Chapter 7 and follow the escape artist. Discovering the new digs of your rotten ex may be as easy as following them from their favorite pool hall or work location to their new pad—which you hope will be a cesspool. However, if they've already dropped out, the mark is looking over their shoulder, so practice good shadowing techniques.

I followed Hans home from the gym. Bingo. But, he wasn't living in a dump. Au contraire. The shit had somehow rented a luxury condo overlooking the ocean. And, since he had never sold one item of software from his nonexistent company, the rent was clearly paid for with Roberta's missing dough.

Search Out Undisclosed Information (Use Chapter 3)

If your mark is a spouse (the reality in 80 percent of my cases), especially from a second or short-term marriage, then you'll be looking for information your better half hasn't disclosed. This would include:

- **Previous marriage**

- **Another residence**

- **Criminal record, maybe from years earlier**

- **Storage facility rental**

- **Aliases or name variations**

Interview Yourself: Answer Questions a Private Eye Would Ask

Every case is different, so it's time to see what information you have that will aid an investigator in pretexting the subject for credit card information, checking out the subject's garbage for an offshore account, or accessing public records to see if your cheating asshole spouse bought an airplane with your life savings.

In addition to collecting the basic information described above, the following are typical questions I always ask a new client seeking assets recovery, particularly in a divorce case, as I build a file on the case. If you're the one building the file, you need to ask them of yourself.

- What was yours or jointly owned that is now missing? Make a list.

- What assets are in the subject's control? Make a list. Your target may well have moved his or her assets out of these accounts, but the trace starts there.

- What's the name and account number of financial institutions where the target has a bank account or you two had a joint account?

- Does the spouse have stocks? Do you know the name of the broker?

- Does the target have an interest in any entities—a corporation, LLC, or DBA (Doing Business As)?

- Can you photocopy the subject's checkbook registers and financial statements? These are important starting points. Even if the accounts have been emptied, the account numbers will be the starting point for a trace.

- Where might your mark most logically try to hide assets? Hans trusted banks. Hey, he was Swiss, after all. A Swiss bank account was a no-brainer. Did Buffy love jewelry? Was Bob a tightass who didn't trust banks? Was George irrationally obsessed with his baseball card collection? Possible hiding places would include:

  - Backyard

  - With relatives, lovers, friends

  - Domestic and/or foreign financial institutions and investments (banks, stocks, funds)

- Domestic and/or foreign corporate and partner-ship holdings

- Domestic and/or foreign real estate vehicle own-ership

- Luxury items (including expensive cars, jewelry, boats, and airplanes)

- Staged lawsuit

- Collectibles

- Do you know your target's insurance agent? Sometimes, a person will hide $20,000 snatched from the joint account and pop it in an annuity where he or she hopes no one will think to look.

- What do you know about the target's address history? If your target doesn't already live with you and you're find-ing the assets on the QT (this is a typical scenario), list what you know about current and previous addresses. The address is the beginning of so many threads to assets discovery.

- Does the subject use any addresses other than the home address, such as a PO box?

- What would the subject buy with his or her newfound wealth?

- What credit cards does the target have? We want to know if he or she has overpaid them to hide cash.

- Do you have a copy of the income tax return? Can you photocopy it for ultimate use by the PI or attorney? This document may offer various things that are important for tracking money.

- Do you have the names of known creditors, so we can see if the target overpaid a mortgage in order to hide the cash?

- Do you have the license tag numbers on vehicles and vessels?

- Has the target done any recent foreign travel? During this session, I always asked the subject this. Although you need a PI and a lawyer to complete a foreign assets investigation, you will want to assemble this information for your pros.

- Who are the subject's friends? If the subject were going to trust someone, who would it be? It's not always a family member. A friend or business partner can be a thread to the subject and the missing stuff.

- If a lover is involved, what's the lover's name and address? If I'm looking for a man, I'll want to know the maiden or previous married names of the lover. In many of my cases, the girlfriend will open a bank account under a previous name to hide her lover's funds for him.

- All known phone numbers? The phone records may indicate calls to a bank in Philadelphia or a stockbroker in Montana that you didn't know about.

If you've determined that there's still something to find, there are three different ways to investigate, and the same is true in the search for proof of assets—a physical hunt, an electronic search, and an investigation in person at the courthouse. Select the approach appropriate to your target and your resources. If you are going to conduct all three, select a logical order based on your target.

THE SEARCH FOR HIDDEN CASH ASSETS

IF YOU HAVE the access to the target's home (if you still live with the jerk and he or she doesn't know you're looking), vehicle, office, or boat, conduct a search for hidden cash and other assets. First and foremost, look for liquid funds that can be located and hopefully recovered. The first rule of hiding money is: Convert everything to cash and put it somewhere new and untraceable. While you're looking for cash, you may also be looking for smaller valuables such as jewelry, coins, small art pieces, and other collectibles. Remember, if you can get your hands on it, it becomes 90 percent yours and now you can hide it—but in a better place.

Find the Loose Cash

Should you conclude that there are some bucks hidden somewhere in your home or on your property and you have access, start there. You need to search your primary residence and second homes. You may want to buy a metal detector for about $80 if you think burying cash in the yard fits the profile of the person trying to do you wrong. Vengeful and emotional adversaries aren't always so slick, so be sure to check the standard places:

- **Under the mattress**

- **Toolbox**

- **Cosmetic case**

- **Freezer**

- **Toilet tank**

- **Under the carpet in corners of rooms**

- **Attics**

- Shed

- Workshop

- Vehicles

- Boats

- Tackle box

- Closets

- Pockets of old jackets

- Briefcases

- Garages

- Battery compartments of electronic devices

- Office

- Homes of friends and relatives

- Gym locker

- Motorcycle saddles

I once found a considerable stash for a client hidden in a fishing boot in the clothes rack at the back of a closet.

In another case, we found $37,000 in cash for the pissed-off wife of a farmer. You'd never assume there was any money there. It was a meager house with a rusting tractor out back. She'd been married thirty-five years to this jerk and finally had enough abuse. She'd served the pig with a restraining order, so he couldn't get on the property. She sent us looking for a gallon jar with a metal lid. Like other farmers who sold vegetables, her husband did a cash business, and as it turns out, a seriously successful one. She believed he'd buried it behind the shed. When our metal detector revealed nothing there, we tore up the farmer's workshop. And there it was. The old jar with the metal lid. At first we thought it was a piece of junk. But it was crammed with twenties, tens, fives and fifties—$37,000 in all. My fee: $1,000. Too late, buddy. You can forget about your jar. She was ecstatic. She never told anyone about finding the money until after the divorce. Otherwise, it would have gone into joint assets.

Roberta's family had no access to Hans's home, sports car, or office (he'd faked the existence of that anyway); but they now had Hans's address, so Roberta's children started with the boy toy's garbage to look for any clues as to where Hans might have parked the loot. He wouldn't have just buried it in the landscaped yard at his condo. He was Swiss, after all. He grew up with banks, not buried coffee tins of money.

Sometimes, extremes are called for, as was one case where I was hired by a law firm on behalf of creditors in a bankruptcy case to find the defendant's assets.

The defendant was a large commercial tomato grower. His crop yield per acre was way below average. Of course, his product was in litigation and the sales were being monitored for the court. Something did not add up. Where was the missing cash going and how? I spent hours on surveillance, but trying to stake out a thousand-acre farm is just about hopeless. The creditors thought that he was bringing in private buyers who were supplying their own labor, picking the fields, and loading the crop into private trucks. He was probably selling for cash and carry only. But there were way too many gates to cover them all. Finally, I rented a helicopter for the day, climbed aboard, and had the pilot buzz the farm. I was able to shoot video of the trucks, including their tag numbers, in the field loading tomatoes. When we later ran the tags and contacted the owners, most denied being at the farm. Once I showed them the tape, however, their story changed and we got the evidence we needed. Still, the defendant did manage to hide several hundred thousand dollars in farm equipment before I was hired, and we never found it. The defendant in this case had farms in several states, under various corporate names.

The point of this story is that sometimes you have to be clever and also willing to spend a few bucks to get the evidence you need. I have used air surveillance before on what we call "hard targets." The chopper was very expensive, but you can go to a small airport and rent a pilot and small plane for about fifty bucks an hour plus fuel. The smaller airports are best to try first. There are many pilots who need to get time logged and welcome a paying chance to do so.

The first step in locating the target's secret bank and investment accounts is locating the institutions and the personal and business account numbers. These you'll be passing on to your attorney so he or she can subpoena the records and/or freeze the accounts.

People tend to do many of their financial dealings at the same place, so second accounts, loans, CDs, mortgages, and credit cards are often linked to this account in the records. This secondary information can, of course, be key to finding other assets, such as property and credit card purchases. All of the following techniques are used by the pros.

Legal Techniques for Discovering Cash in Bank Accounts

Although you can spend a hefty sum having your attorney send blanket subpoenas throughout the area where your target lives or hire a PI to find the information for a minimum of about $400, you can try to find the missing bank accounts yourself first.

You need the account numbers for your attorney to freeze the account where you suspect your loot has been hidden and to subpoena bank statements.

Call the Water Company Collections Department

Contact the water company to see if a bank account exists under the target's name. This is one method I use often to find a mark's bank accounts. Try the collections division. It's legal for them to release it. They don't have to, but they have never turned me down.

Give the Mark a Check

If the mark runs or owns a business or service operation, have someone purchase something from the mark's store or business or hire the mark to perform a service. Be sure to pay with a check. Bingo. The cancelled check will provide you with the financial institution account number right on the back. Now you know where the mark has a business account and, perhaps, personal accounts and loans.

Request a Rent Check from the Landlord

You have nothing to lose by asking a current or previous landlord—especially if the target has skipped—for banking information. Ask to see the rental application, the cancelled check for the security deposit, or a rent payment check.

The Money-Order Ploy

Here's a shot that sometimes works, and it's a lot cheaper than paying a PI $375 to do a bank search. Buy a $25 money order at a convenience store, then make it out to the target from a made-up organization. It might be from the Neighborhood Watch Committee or some other group you've invented for this purpose. That's the beauty of money orders. They can be from anyone to anyone.

Next, mail it to the mark with no explanation and save the stub. Go back to the place you purchased it in about a month. Claim the person never got it and request a copy of the front and back of the money order. The copy will cost you $8 and will take about two weeks to get. Bingo. You may well discover the mark's bank account if he or she deposited it or cashed it at a bank.

The Uniform Commercial Code (UCC) Filing

Go to the secretary of state's office website and type in the various names used by your target. If your mark is a creditor or debtor for a commercial loan of over $5,000, you'll find a wealth of information on your target's financial institutions and assets.

In this file, you'll find an application that will list banks and account numbers, financial statements, and the names of creditors such as banks, finance companies, and private lenders.

The Department of Revenue

This state department of revenue office is also, in some states, referred to as the sales tax office. As you cannot access this online, you must go to the state capitol or to a branch office, which is usually located in a major population center in your county. Here you can check to see if the mark has a permit to collect sales tax and you can often get a copy of their application.

This will list a lot of useful information regarding the target's business operations, the business location, the corporate FEIN number, the banking institution for the business, and even a checking account and bank location. If he or she has failed to pay the sales tax, you may even find a tax warrant for the mark in these files. Any of these pieces of data can be the starting point for a thread leading to a hidden asset.

Dumpster Diving

Some investigative agencies such as the FBI, IRS, local law enforcement agencies, and private investigators will do trash searches. The information obtained will reveal the bank where the mark has an account in addition to lots of personal information about the mark and his or her habits. A trash search tells a lot about a person. The subject's whole life goes in that garbage can: medications to junk mail, bank statements to bills, and even what brand of beer he or she drinks. You can try this on yourself for a week and write down what you learn about yourself based on the trash. I assure you, you will seriously consider buying a shredder soon!

Roberta's family found several bank accounts listed for Hans by contacting the water company and by going through his garbage. They also discovered that he got mail for someone named Rolf with the same last name. This was useful information because it meant Hans used different names.

They got the name of one local bank on one of the coffee-stained envelopes in Hans's trash. There was no bank statement, but at least there was the name of a financial institution. Of course, what we hadn't counted on was the fact that Hans's respect for banking came from growing up in his hometown, Zurich, the Mecca of private banking. They also found two empty envelopes with return addresses in Switzerland, an international phone number with the country code on a scrap piece of paper, and the ripped half of a page with half of the number of an electronic wire and bank routing number.

In addition, there was an issue of an enthusiast's Mustang magazine; a receipt for a storage-facility rental, one known for high security storage boxes such as you'd rent for jewelry; and a prepaid credit card statement showing charges for thousands of dollars, including a Rolex watch, a spa membership, and a charge for a $225 haircut.

The Fake Entity Ruse

This is another elaborate, but very useful, PI trick to obtain banking information. To perform this ruse, you need to get a checking account in the name of an entity you make up. To accomplish this, you will create and register a fake entity with which you can run several games on your mark to get him or her to give up their own bank account number.

With the new laws, the bank requires proof—such as a FEIN number—that the name on the account represents a legal entity. Ergo, you must create a legal fake entity with a name. Choose a name that matches the ploy you're going to use. There are two ways to legally register your "new business" with the secretary of state's office.

The first is to open a corporation for a few hundred dollars and get a FEIN number. This is too expensive unless you've got multiple targets. For much less, you can file and register a fictitious named business and then set up a checking account. This is called a DBA (Doing Business As) entity. With proof that your entity is legal, you can open an account. Instead of waiting for the printed checks to arrive by snail mail, use an inexpensive computer program kit that will allow you to print your checks immediately (around $30). Now employ any one of the following ploys with your new checks.

THE CHECK GUARANTEE ASSOCIATION PLOY. Using the covert business you've just created and registered, you can contact the Check Guarantee Association, which gives you a phone number that you can call to discover if a check is good. It's all verbal over the phone. Using the institution's name, you explain, "I have a check from Susie Wilson for $780, and I want to know if it's good." They will have a list of all banks and history as well as whether the account holder's check will be covered. Often, they'll give you additional bank account numbers.

THE REFUND PLOYS. You send fake refund, rebate, or thank-you checks to the target from your fake entity. When he or she cashes the check, bingo. You've hopefully got your target's bank and account number. Or, send a letter to the target's address with a check for $15. Describe this as a refund on a purchase. The check is from your fake entity such as Consumer Rebate, Inc. In the letter, reference a "recent purchase" that may have been made by your mark: dish soap, paper towels, or toothpaste. You know the brands.

Thank-You-for-Shopping Ploy. Enclosing a check for $25 from your made-up DBA—say, the "Florida Marketing Refund Association"—include a note: "Thank you for shopping at (insert popular store here). The Florida Marketing Refund Association is authorized to thank you for shopping in our state. Enclosed you will find a $25 shopper's refund. Thank you for supporting our community." You can also offer a thank you for shopping at a major department store or drugstore that you know is used by your target.

Good-Citizen-Refund Ploy. Send a letter from Insurance Adjustments, Inc. saying, "Our records indicate you're entitled to a safe-driver refund. Thank you for practicing safety on our public roadways. Please see the check enclosed." You may also send a "refund" from the National Clean Highways Committee thanking the target for "maintaining a clean neighborhood."

Get the Bank Account Numbers by Subpoena

Once things are in the courts, you can also get the bank account numbers through the subpoena process. But you must outsmart your opponent. By the time things are under legal jurisdiction, the original and known accounts will be empty—unless the person who put your missing money there is a complete idiot.

But, you can also request that your lawyer subpoena several documents and sources which may hold the key to your target's banking information.

Remember, when you conduct an assets recovery, you're really working for your lawyer, collecting, among other things, legal targets from which to subpoena records. Instead of paying a PI to do it, you've collected the names of landlords and banks, and employers and insurance agents yourself. Your lawyer then uses this information to get official documents through subpoena power. It's not at all uncommon for the client to suggest subpoena targets to his or her lawyer.

Previous or Current Landlord

You can subpoena the previous or current landlord for a copy of the rental application, security deposit, and rent checks to see where the mark banked. Most people are usually creatures of habit. Once a banking relationship is established, it generally remains the same.

Current or Past Employer

If you know the mark's employer, you may consider serving a Business Record Subpoena on the employer to obtain a copy of a payroll check the mark has cashed. The check should have the mark's account number and possibly the name of the bank on the back of it.

The Mark's Deposition

At this proceeding, you can demand that the mark tell you where his bank account is. The unfortunate effect of this procedure is that the mark can take most (if not all) of his money out of the account before you can get to it. However, do not dismiss the usefulness of the examination too quickly. Not all marks are Einsteins. Some ex-wives and ex-employers do not think to empty their bank accounts. Additionally, there is actual value in finding a bank account with only a few bucks in it or even one that has already been closed. The value is in the microfilmed records the bank will retain on the account.

Think about it for a second. What documents would a mark deposit in his or her bank account? How about a payroll check, the spouse's payroll check, stock-dividend checks, and rental-income checks. Each category of information is extremely valuable to a creditor enforcing a judgment.

What is more, the mark will probably take the funds from his now-defunct account and—probably in the form of a check from his old account—deposit it in a new account.

The UCC Filing

If you found a UCC filing on the secretary of state's website (see above), revealing that your target is a creditor (secured party) or debtor on a commercial loan, you can issue several subpoenas that could produce a hidden bank-account number.

SUBPOENA A CHECK FROM THE CREDITOR TO THE MARK. In a loan situation, the bank will issue a check to the mark. The mark will deposit the check in his or her bank account. As the check makes its way back to the issuing bank, the mark's bank-account number will be on the back of the check issued by the bank. If you subpoena the secured party for a copy of this check, it will show the document trail, including the name and account number of the bank in which the mark actually deposited the check.

In addition, ask your attorney to subpoena the targeted bank for any loan applications and/or financial statements of the mark, any checks the bank issued to the mark, and the mark's checks for loan payments.

Fish for Bank Accounts with Blanket Subpoenas

Based on all known addresses, ask your lawyer to issue a blanket subpoena in all domestic locations (counties and cities) and foreign cities. You may also base the blanket subpoena on return addresses on envelopes you found in the target's trash. If you know the subject traveled to Barbados in the past few years, ask the lawyer to try the blanket subpoena there. The government may or may not recognize the United States subpoena, but it's worth a try. It's up to the lawyer to determine which countries will cooperate. The blanket subpoena is a technique often used by the IRS.

Look for Money Stashed in Other People's Accounts

Many bird-dogs, trying to take possession of it all, hide money by putting it in the account of a relative or friend. This is much more difficult to recover. Your greedy ex or coked-out business partner will allege the money was deposited in that account as the repayment of a loan. So your mark may have already plunked the money you two made together into the account of a friend, a lover, a sister, a parent, a child, or a complete stranger he met in a bar that afternoon.

In one case, a jerk named "Fred" skipped out on his wife and kids, taking everything in their joint checking and savings accounts with him. The wife hired us to discover where he went and, more important, to show her the money. When we revealed the name of her husband's lover to our client, she recognized the name right away. "Tina" appeared in the company records as an employee. This hussy had a great job. She didn't work. She lived in a different county over 130 miles away. For over two years, she'd been depositing a paycheck for $800 a month just for sitting on her ass in a paid-for apartment.

And if the subject claims that putting money in someone else's account was to repay a loan or some other legal transaction, there's often little you can do to prove otherwise or recover it. But you still want to find it. Unfortunately, you may have no authority to claim this money. All you'll find out are the frustrating facts about where the money resides. Still, it's worth pursuing. Here's what you can try:

- Consult the list you made when you set up your file of friends or relatives whom the mark might trust with the loot.

- Using the same methods from the water company to the refund ploys, find the bank account number for the people on this list. Your target may have foolishly listed himself or herself as joint on this new account.

Using the bank-fraud pretext with the girlfriend (no longer legal—see Chapter 6), we uncovered that the cheating jerk Fred and his "employee" Tina had a joint account with thousands of dollars of skip money in it. They'd been planning this for two years.

When confronted by my client's lawyer, Fred had trouble defining Tina's role in the company. "Squeeze" was not a standard job description in a construction outfit. They subpoenaed the hussy and, with a straight face, asked what her duties were. The husband had to count the money sent to his girlfriend as "assets" in the divorce.

Hunt Down Stocks and Bonds

The only stock information you can find as a nonprofessional will be at www.hooversonline.com or www.edgar.com. At these sites, type in names and aliases and you'll have limited free searches to learn the major investors in stocks, bonds, and mutual funds. Mostly, you can find listings of major stockholders of listed corporations that are members of the U.S. Securities and Exchange Commission. For example, you can find out that Joe Smith owns 25 percent of the stock for a major computer company. You'll find a sales record of his buying more or selling shares.

For smaller fish, you'll hope to get from trash retrieval brokerage accounts, names of brokers, or names of brokerage firms that your attorney can subpoena. Again, full disclosure of what's concealed in these accounts will require a subpoena, but you won't know to ask your attorney to serve the firm a subpoena unless you discover your target has an account there. This is an example of legwork you can do before your lawyer goes on the clock.

Locate Credit Card Accounts

You're hoping to find the number and types of credit cards held by your target so your attorney can subpoena the records to see, for example, if your ex is hiding cash assets by overpaying credit card accounts. Unless you have access to statements or are joint on the account, you're not likely to know if Buffy purchased a mink unless you see her wearing it or your lawyer subpoenas the records. Your options are: going through the target's trash and performing a pretext on the subject to locate this information for your attorney.

Pretext the Subject for a Credit Card Number

See the rules of performing a pretext in previous chapters. If the mark will recognize you, use a friend to make the call or purchase a voice changer. Based on your target's interests, offer the mark a deal over the phone that will get him or her to give up a credit card. Example: "Our records indicate that you purchased a Toshiba laptop. This month we're offering a travel charger for $3 that you can use on a plane. Would you like to put that on your Visa or MasterCard? We also take Discover and American Express." To establish credibility, I pretend I'm from another city. If calling Florida, I pretend I'm from Philadelphia. "How's your weather down there? Have you survived the hurricanes?"

SEARCH FOR PHYSICAL ASSETS IN PUBLIC RECORDS

NOW, WE'RE READY to look for real estate and other noncash assets that might be registered but hidden from view under a layer of corporate secrecy. To conduct this final step, we need to use all the names we have gathered in our file: all name variations of the target, aliases, names of trusts, names of businesses, and names of entities under which assets could be hiding.

Search for Asset Shelters

One critical avenue for assets recovery is looking for property and other assets that have been hidden under the cloak of a business or corporation. You will want to complete this part of the search before you look for the actual stuff—the houses, the racehorses, the yachts. They won't likely be registered at the tax collector's office under your target's given name. Although people choose to place assets in business entities for the tax advantages, creation of a secret entity is one method people use to hide assets from you. The person concealing assets from you could be hiding them right under your nose if you don't know where to look.

Secretary of State's Office Website

The secretary of state's office is the first stop, but rather than going to the state capitol, you will want to do this search online. The search string equals the state name followed by "secretary of state," i.e. New York Secretary of State.

Lots of big-ticket items, including real estate, art, airplanes, and luxury items, can be secreted under a corporate name or a business name. On the secretary of state's website, go to all of the different selections on the menu where your target might have an interest—and thus a yacht registered. Look for corporations, Limited Liability Corporations (LLCs), DBAs (Doing Business As), and Limited Partnerships. Each type of entity has a separate database, and you will want to choose each one from the menu for a separate search. Legally, you must register all entities, so whether they are legitimate businesses which your target is hiding or a made-up asset shelter, it will be registered here under state law.

DIVISION OF CORPORATIONS. You can research this two ways, either by the name of the person or the name of the corporation. Using the names, name variations, and aliases of your target, do an "officer search," which will return any corporations in which your target is an officer. You will need the names of all of these corporations where your subject may be concealing his assets by registering them under these various entities.

FICTITIOUS BUSINESS NAMES (DBAs). Besides doing a corporate search, on the same website, look for businesses that may be owned by your target that are legal but not incorporated. Search (click) on Fictitious Business Names to see if your mark has registered a business with the secretary of state. The owner is "doing business as" the name. If your target is running a DBA, the name will appear. Names such as Joe's Tire Service or Ginny's Cleaning Company would be typical. These are businesses that are not incorporated and have what are known as "legal fictitious names." Complete the same process for the other entities on the menu including Limited Liability Corporations and Limited Liability Partnerships.

UCC (Uniform Commercial Code) Website

The UCC records are another source for assets discovery available in the secretary of state's public records. Put fictitious, known, and corporate names on this screen one by one and any asset in excess of five grand for which your target has a secured interest or indebtedness will show up. Any time we buy something worth more than $5,000 and get or make a loan on it, we have to register the loan showing what equipment is secured on that loan and how much the note is for. This will include heavy manufacturing tools and machinery, farm equipment, vehicles, and construction equipment (cement mixers and bulldozers).

City and County Occupational Licensing

Armed with fictitious, corporate, and known alias names, check city and county occupational licensing for additional information about the target's business interests. You will need to show up in person to city hall for the city licensing bureau and the county administration building for county licensing bureaus. You're requesting a copy of your target's application for licensing, which will tell you how long the business has been established, whom the previous owner was, and the names of other contact persons and business associates. Because you need a state license to get a local license, the file will also give you state licensing verification. Most businesses have to have state and local licenses. Although it differs from state to state and county and county, most businesses need a state license to qualify for local businesses.

At this office, we found out that the business our target incorporated, called Concept 2000, is actually a real estate office. The records here also give us more names of people who might know something about our subject. In the file are listed all applications for each year, current and previous business partners, including a disgruntled former partner who will tell us all about the cattle ranch out in Texas and apartment building in Louisiana. These records might give you managers, address of the business, number of employees, and business principles (partners). This file also may include whether the target owns the business, the buildings, the fixtures, the equipment, and sometimes, other assets like condos or boats.

Online Search for Hidden Real Estate Assets

You would most likely know if your spouse owns any real estate, but if you're looking for the assets of a lover, ex-partner, distant relative, or legal adversary, you will certainly want to locate these assets.

For currently owned property, you may need to know the county where you believe your target owns property. Although there are Internet statewide property sites for many states, all states have countywide databases.

One of my favorite links is publicrecordssearch.com, which is different than the site I mentioned in Chapter 3, www.publicrecordsfinder.com. However, that site could be used as well. This is a company that does in-depth public records recovery, but they also provide a page of free searches by category for each individual state. An example of this is if you were looking for something in the state of Florida, you would click on the Florida link and the page will open with links that include every county clerk's office online.

Under the Florida link, for example, you can select from an alphabetical list of every county clerk's office in your state that is providing free records online. Simply click on the county of your choice and when the page opens, you will have a square to place the target's first and last name. When you select Official Records, a screen will appear of everyone matching the last name and variations of the first name (Edward Jones, Edwina Jones, Edwin Jones). Most don't provide a place to insert a middle initial in the search, but look carefully at the middle initial for the hits that appear for a match with your subject.

In this phase of the search, you will find listed the transaction history of any properties the person has bought or sold, along with what they may currently own. Reading these pages is sometimes confusing. As an example, the screen will use initials to indicate a type of transaction. Instead of the word "deed," the screen displays "d." On these websites, there's a master guide which tells you what those initials mean—for example, "wt" for warranty deed or "qd" for quick claim deed. This will vary from state to state, so print out the guide.

If your target is married, don't forget to do a search on the wife's previous married names and maiden name if you know them. In some cases, you will also want to use nicknames. If there is nothing under Michael, look under Mike. Chuck-Charles, Ted-Theodore. You get the picture. It depends on what they called themselves on the deed.

This is an area where many private investigators fail because they don't take the time to do these various combination searches. Almost anyone that's computer savvy today can run a property search; however, you have to be a thinker and play the long shots in order to do a thorough job. That's why we make the big bucks.

You must also run a search string under any known business, because some people put their property under a business or corporate umbrella. These are not official records for court that you're copying, but critical information your lawyer can use to find the legal documents.

Search the County Clerk Recorder's Office

Of course, if you don't have computer access or need the actual real estate transaction records, you can find more complete files at the county courthouse. In most courthouses, these records will be found in the clerk of courts division, also known as the county recorder's office in some states (this is the same office I mentioned in Chapter 3). A simple phone call ahead of time will give you the correct name of the division you need to locate these property records. What you're looking for is the book and page number in the Official Records Book (OR), the parties involved in the property transaction, and the date of the transaction. In most courthouses today, one of three systems for storing and thus "initial retrieval" are computer, microfiche, and microfilm.

The most prominent method is the computer console with several computer stations, and next to them, a brief set of instructions. These instructions will vary according to the software used in your state or county. Simply follow the instructions and conduct your search on the keyboard, which will then display a screen of entries. Normally, there is print capability for a cost per page, but not always, so have a pen and notebook. Pray that your county is electronically current. The lines are sometimes three hours long in Broward County, Florida, for example, because the records aren't on computer.

In some computer systems, you simply click on the image icon, which will show you the complete document and you can simply hit

Print. These documents are of various sizes, from one page to unlimited pages. Only print what you absolutely need, as most clerks' offices charge one dollar per page for these records. If the system you're using does not have a print option, you will then take your information to the nearest clerk who will access the actual file and photocopy the actual document.

A lot of privacy laws prevent the actual image of the original document from being displayed on the Internet, although you are provided with an accurate text of information. If you're just doing an assets search, the listing will be sufficient. If you need this as evidence, you need to stand in line for a "certified copy" of an actual document. This means that at the time you make your purchase from the clerk, you need to request a "certified copy," not just a copy. And, yes, the bad news is, it's three dollars a page for a certified record because the clerk has to stand up out of the chair. Records are big business.

In public-records work, you'll also discover trusts. You'll commonly find this when doing a property search. Mike Jones owned a house and deeded it over to the Jones Family Trust. This is an excellent way to hide real estate assets and, for you, the pursuer, an excellent way to find them.

Local Property Tax Assessor's Office

In Florida, the tax collector's office is also in charge of vehicle and boat registration renewals, but this may not be the same in all states. Other states will have vehicles separate. Here you're looking for two things: all items requiring a registration that may be parked at a girlfriend's condo; and a follow-up on our earlier search for property records. Again, use all the names and aliases of persons and entities under which assets could be listed. Conduct a search for registrations for cars, motorcycles, mobile homes, RVs, trailers, jet skis, and boats.

Armed with what you just found in the clerk of court's records, in the tax collector's office, you're confirming what you found in the courthouse and looking for other properties. You can see how you often need to move back and forth between different government entities and different kinds of records. You sometimes work forward and then go into reverse to complete a thorough property search.

First, run your subject's name and all names associated with him or her through the tax collector's property database to see if the tax collector has a match of the mailing address and name to which tax notices are sent to your subject. And if he does, you then match the parcel numbers on those tax notices to the ones you found in county records or online. Incidentally, the actual tax notice will have appraised value, delinquencies, property description, date of construction, and history of how many years your subject has paid taxes on it (and thus owned it).

Here you want to record in your notebook any names to which the tax notices were sent. Let's say you're doing an assets search on your ex-partner who claims he lost a large chunk of the shared profits gambling. You're not so sure he didn't just hide it. You match the property number for his home which you found in the county records against the tax payment history. You see a notice went to C and L Properties. You didn't know to look for that name before. You've discovered a new name used by that thieving rogue who took all the shared profits from your lawn-care service.

Back to the Courthouse

Now it's back to the courthouse to do a records search on C and L Properties. There you'll get the OR (official record) and see that this property was sold to C and L by a person who happens to be the wife of your former sleazeball partner. You've worked forward and then gone into reverse.

Find Big-Ticket Luxury Items: Boats and Airplanes

Boats: Coast Guard Website

You are required to register a boat over five tons with the Coast Guard as a "documented vessel." If you don't check here, you might miss a major hidden asset: You could miss a $5 million vessel. This could be the forty-foot Morgan sailboat that Buffy would have bought had the kids not caught her.

Boats under five tons are registered at the tag office or registered with the Coast Guard as a documented vessel. To hide a boat purchase, a sneaky person might skip the country and register on the federal level, where a pursuer may not look. At a certain size, it's cheaper to go through the federal government than the state for registration.

On the other hand, if big money is at stake, your ex may have plunked the cash into a big boat, just like Buffy tried to do. Go to the site for the Coast Guard where you can run vessel ownership by vessel name, registration number, or corporate or owner name.

Airplanes: FAA Database

The best way to find out about whether your target owns a plane: Do a free online search at the Federal Aviation Administration (FAA) under the Bureau of Aviation website (www.faa.gov/).

Blackbookonline

This is my favorite site (www.blackbookonline.com) to see if my target owns any planes or documented vessels. The owner of the site publishes a pocket-sized book every year, called *The Investigator's Little Black Book* by Robert Scott, which has a wealth of Internet links updated yearly. You can buy it at the local bookstore, and you'll find one of these in every private investigator's office, including my own. The online site, which is actually a promotion for the book, has a link for documented vessels and planes.

Collectibles

The smart money is on the sneak who hides assets in collectibles. This is very common because these assets are the most difficult to trace and recover. Leaving aside the failure of Beanie Babies, you might, for example find your scoundrel partner has put the business earnings in:

- Art

- Baseball cards

- Stamps

- Coins

- Antiques

- Guns

- Civil War swords

- Comic books

- First-edition books

- Memorabilia

Ask yourself, what is the subject's interest and expertise? With coins, you'll want to talk to the local coin dealer to see if your ex sold a collection that was supposed to be community property or hid loose cash by purchasing one. For baseball cards, you'll want to go to eBay or any place that auctions sports memorabilia. Google and eBay are as good as places as any to look for coin and stamp markets. You might find an eBay ad for your stuff that your spouse is selling. There, you'll also see a history of buying and selling, including a list of persons who have purchased vintage comic books or a stamp collection.

If you think your target is hiding cash in a stamp collection and you find the rat's name on a list, you can contact the seller for amounts and objects and, if the buyer paid by check, ask to look at the back of the check. The amounts and timing could well figure into your settlement.

Several years ago, I was hired to find the assets of a spouse whose wife accused him of hiding some very expensive collectible baseball cards from their joint property. The wife knew he had them, but he denied it, saying they "must have been stolen." When he thought he was safe after the divorce, he took some of the cards to a shop and cashed them in for $10,000. I showed his picture to the shop owner, who recognized the man and gave me copies of the transaction. We turned this over to the lawyer who went after the cash. However, the rest of the cards never surfaced. The husband denied he had them, and the wife could never prove it.

That's the beauty of things like coins and cards. There's no paper trail. But that's the next chapter.

Meanwhile, Hans was smart enough to hide the money and most of his assets overseas. It was an expensive lesson. All Roberta was left with was the contents of Hans's storage locker that her lawyer was able to seize, which amounted to a little under $5,000, nowhere near the half a million he got away with. However, at least the family was able to save quite a bit of money by doing much of the legwork themselves.

SIX

COVER YOUR ASSETS

TO HIDE YOUR assets, you not only have to outsmart the person after you—the person who may be reading Chapter 5 of this book— but you have to outsmart me, the private eye hired by your adversaries to find and seize your assets. Consider the following statistics and tidbits:

FAVORITE TAX HAVEN: Dubai

CORPORATE INCOME TAX OF DUBAI: None

WITHHOLDING TAX OF DUBAI: None

IMPORT DUTY OF DUBAI: None

ONE NIGHT IN A ONE-BEDROOM SUITE AT DUBAI'S BURJ AL ARAB HOTEL: $1,116

MAXIMUM AMOUNT OF CASH THAT CAN BE MOVED AT ONE TIME TO AN OFFSHORE ACCOUNT: $10,000

RESTRICTIONS ON MOVING CHECKS OR MONEY ORDERS TO OFFSHORE
ACCOUNTS: NONE

COST OF OPENING AN OFFSHORE ACCOUNT: $250

DOCUMENTS IN ADDITION TO A PHOTO ID NEEDED TO OPEN AN OFFSHORE
ACCOUNT: 0

COST FOR EACH INTERNATIONAL ATM TRANSACTION FROM YOUR
INTERNATIONAL OFFSHORE BANK: Sfr.3 (US $4)

INCOME TAX LIABILITY FOR OFFSHORE ASSETS: None

NUMBER OF COUNTRIES HAVING OFFSHORE BANKING SYSTEMS: 69

NUMBER OF UNITED STATES LAWS FOR REGULATING OFFSHORE ACCOUNTS: 5

NUMBER OF REGULATIONS FOR OFFSHORE BANKING AFTER 2001 USA PATRIOT
ACT: 2

TYPICAL COST INVOLVED IN LEGALLY HIDING ASSETS: High

COST OF CONSULTING A PI ABOUT HIDING ASSETS: $1,200 to $8,000

While 10 percent of my clients come to me looking for someone else's hidden cache, about 5 percent are looking for advice on how to hide assets from the 10 percent trying to find them. From whom might you want to keep your assets private? Think about it: creditors; ex-spouses; a current lover; government snoops; prying relatives; a prospective spouse; nosy acquaintances; or a past, current, or prospective business partner.

Again, I don't judge. Although I know how to do it, I will not, of course, provide a client or the reader of this book with advice that could lead to illegal activities such as embezzlement or tax evasion. But there's no law against hiding assets that are yours. You can hire my firm to advise you on the ways to protect your assets from greedy relatives, collection agencies, and other private investigators, or you can do it yourself.

"Frank Brown" came to me with a complicated business dissolution, and he wanted to save a piece of his ass in the process. He didn't tell me how much money he had, just that he wanted to protect some of it. To hide his assets, we had to analyze what form they were in. He had CDs, a small brokerage-firm account, and like anyone else in business, a lump of cash at home. (He never reported cash clients, and had several thousand there.) He'd been doing well over the years, saving for his children's college education and his retirement. He was a shy, unassuming guy who had been married to his high school sweetheart.

His business partner (and backer) of his two-year-old business suspected the cash stash existed, but she didn't know how much or where it was. That's right, a *she*. His backer was a trust-fund baby and midlife crisis named "Trixie."

Trixie had been turned on by the butt crack peeking through Frank's jeans when he fixed a wiring problem at her lakefront home. She invited him to stay for coffee, screwed his brains out, paid for him to divorce his high school sweetheart, installed him in her condo in town, and set him up in his own electrical company. When he came to me, Frank had seen the light and was going back to his wife. Trixie was pissed, and wanted to ruin him if she could.

Frank had a lot of assets he wanted to keep or pass on to his kids. And now Trixie was after them. We helped Frank, charging him about seventy hours of work at $75 per hour. But, you can use the steps we took, as outlined in this chapter, and save yourself the money. You will need to read carefully about what can be done legally, always checking with your own local and state laws—sometimes consulting a lawyer. But you can do a lot of the footwork to reduce the amount of time (read: money) your attorney will need to spend on your case.

And get going. Assets protection is time sensitive. The sooner you take any of the steps in this chapter, the better you can protect your estate in the present and the future. If you haven't broached the subject of divorce yet, but you feel that your partner is plotting an escape—or you are—start now and outsmart your future pursuer. The more you plan ahead, the more assets you can save for yourself.

PREEMPT AN ASSAULT ON YOUR ASSETS

TRIXIE'S LAWYER HAD a PI on the trail within four hours after Frank split with her, but he had already planned ahead, taking the steps outlined in this chapter. But, you can't do much if legal proceedings are underway. That would be illegal. You must take these steps before any papers are filed and you are served. Frank did all this before Trixie was on to him and started court action against him. It's true. Possession is 90 percent of the law. Don't be left holding the other 10 percent.

Take Action Before any Legal Action

You need to preserve your assets before the rules of discovery apply. Prior to court action taking place, all assets are considered community marital property. In other words, whoever wipes out the joint account, moves the boat to the Bahamas, and sells the coin collection first, is in the driver's seat.

I once had a client, a seventy-two-year-old man, who had married a thirty-two-year-old belly dancer. He'd been married one month and realized he'd made a mistake. He had met her at a lingerie shop five years earlier, set her up in an apartment, and married her two months after his wife died. Now, it was my job to help him secure his assets against the dancer's litigation and sharp lawyers before she knew she needed to hire them. In his case, there was a lot of money involved.

Before he served the divorce papers and she finally realized she was going to be out on her ass, we had his money in a major offshore corporation with considerable ready cash on hand in a spot so secret that the likelihood of anyone finding it was slim to none.

The cost involved for discovery to an offshore island is considerable. What are the chances of the belly dancer getting all of that cash recovered out of Guernsey with her exotic dancing salary? Zero. My client was counting on that.

Read Chapters 4 and 5

Remove yourself from the public records as outlined in Chapter 4. If someone can find you in any public records, they have a shot at tracing the assets you want to protect. Carefully review Chapter 5. It's just good business to review the places where your adversaries are going to be searching for your cash, the ways and places that someone could find your stuff. And don't put it there.

Dispose of Your Trash Properly

I have solved more cases from the garbage can than any other method. I cannot stress this enough. Your entire life goes into that garbage can. If you expect any kind of privacy, you have to tend to the trash at all times. You can burn it, shred it, bury it, or hide it. But, if you fail to take care of this one single aspect of exposure, I will find your assets. I will nail you, the IRS will nail you, and your ex will nail you. All the money spent on lawyers, trusts, corporations, and offshore accounts will go down the drain.

This is a basic method private investigators and others use to find out secret information, including receipts, phone numbers, credit card statements, bank envelopes, phone bills, etc. See Appendix 3: The Art of Dumpster Diving. If you're setting your life out on the curb, I will know all about you. Why do you put your most private papers at the curb for the whole world to legally peruse and acquire?

Even if you have no legal threats in your life, it makes sense to protect yourself against identity and asset theft. There are people in this society, whom I call "scanners," who spend their time looking for opportunities from which they can steal your identity. The trash is a primary source. To protect yourself from this type of discovery, get a paper shredder and start using it immediately.

Set Aside Enough Cash for a Good Lawyer

We have the best justice system money can buy. Even though you're going to do a lot of work yourself, be sure you have the funds to hire a lawyer if litigation is imminent (divorce, civil suits, business dissolution, etc.).

In my experience, one of the first things a lawyer wants to know is if you can pay. Those who have the cash to pay a lawyer, rule. If you only have a $25,000 or a $50,000 problem, you'll be turned down by a lot of lawyers.

Convert All Assets into Cash

As soon as you know someone is snooping around your financial profile and may try to get their hands on your cash, immediately convert all money assets—such as bank accounts and stocks—to raw cash and then place it somewhere untraceable. Once converted to cash and in your possession, the paper trail is broken, and it's your word against anyone else's where it went. You can say you lost it at the horse track, or that you paid back some loans. Just get all money in your name out of discoverable sources. Three quick moves to protect your assets from prying investigators are:

- **Close all existing financial accounts, such as checking and savings accounts, stocks, bonds and mutual funds**

- **Freeze credit cards**

- **Remove items and cash from the safe deposit box**

BURY YOUR TREASURE: HIDE CASH AND SMALL VALUABLES IN YOUR YARD

YOU NEED TO have access to cash, and there's lots of hiding places for cash and valuable stuff. You won't be collecting interest, but at least you'll have access to it and no one will know where it is. The following are some suggested hiding places to stash your cash.

Personal Home and Property

THE HOLLOW DOOR OR BASEBOARD. It's always comfortable to have cash on hand, but you must choose the proper hiding places for long-term storage and emergency funds. One of the best is a doorway in a residence. A hollow door will hold as much as $500,000 in hundreds dollar bills.

Cut a slot in the top of a hollow core door and drop cash, coins (wrapped in foam), and valuables into the door. Once you've done that, you can fill the hole at the top with wood putty. No one can tell. This is one of the safest places to put valuables. A burglar seldom thinks to look inside of the door itself.

We helped our client with the greedy belly dancer remove the baseboards on the sink basin in his condo and put stacks of wrapped bills behind that.

SPARE TIRE IN A VEHICLE. You can store a lot of money inside a spare tire. Deflate the tire, put in the cash, air it back up, and stow it in your car or truck. No one will look there, and you've got your stash with you. At least you know where it is. You can also fit some doubloons, jewelry, or cash inside the air breather on your car depending on the year and model.

SEALED PVC PIPE BURIED NEXT TO FENCE. Fill a 6-inch piece of PVC pipe with cash, valuable coins, jewelry, doubloons, etc. Cap both ends. Next, dig a fence-post hole beside the posts of an existing fence. Drop in the sealed pipe and replace the carefully cut sod. A fence usually contains a lot of metal, which will prevent a metal detector from finding your stash. The metal fence will set off a false alarm.

After Frank realized Trixie was a mistake, he followed our advice and stashed some of his cash in the spare tire of his truck.

A Rental Storage Facility

A rental facility is an excellent place to store cash or larger assets, including vintage cars and paintings. There is no database for storage facilities, so you'd need a platoon of agents searching everywhere to find the facility where your locker is located. And then most places won't divulge names of the tenants for their storage lockers, even if someone found the one you use. Some people go to another city to rent a locker, just in case they might be spotted.

The only way someone might discover that you have rented a storage locker and/or its location and number is if they found a receipt going through your garbage.

In one case I had several years ago, I was working for the husband gathering information on his soon-to-be-ex wife. He confided in me that during the marriage he had been selling something other than office supplies. He and his ex had accumulated quite a nice fund for a rainy day, which they had hidden aboard their 50-foot motor yacht where he was now living; the wife had gained control of the residence along with temporary support.

He had been prepared to let her have the home and the martial assets until now. One night, after returning from a wild night out with the boys, he went to replenish his pocket cash and found he had been cleaned out. He led me into the main bathroom on the boat to show me where the money had been stashed. He opened the medicine-cabinet door, removed two small screws, and lifted the entire medicine cabinet out of the wall. It took less than three minutes to do. In the hollow area behind the medicine cabinet was a nice storage area where he had kept his cash. Only he and his wife had known about the location. It had been an ingenious hiding place.

Now he had lost over a quarter-million dollars in cash, and he was certain his estranged wife was the culprit. He certainly could not go to the police due to the illegal nature of the income. But he was determined instead to make the divorce a bitter fight just to get some payback. The lesson here is, move the stash if anyone else knows where it is.

Soon after, his wife had a run of bad luck. While I was tailing her, she left a bar very intoxicated. Someone from the bar called the police, and she was arrested for DUI. While she was in jail, someone broke into her home, the home she had once been sharing with my client (in case you're wondering, I didn't do the break-in, which would have been illegal, nor do I advise anyone to do so). Only a few items were taken, but the police found the medicine cabinet in her bathroom on the floor where it had been removed. She had used the same place to hide the cash in the home as in the yacht.

I later saw my former client and he seemed to be in very good spirits, like the proverbial cat who swallowed the canary, and said his divorce was going well. I just smiled as he paid his bill for my surveillance and thought about how things often come full circle.

TO PROTECT YOUR ASSETS, FADE FROM SIGHT

IF YOU CHANGE addresses before you're served with any court order, you haven't violated the law. Since almost all assets can be tracked by computer and all threads lead to a central file, you need to cut off the search for hidden money and other assets at your address. To hide your assets, you need to hide yourself. Move to an unknown address. If process servers can't find you, they can't serve you with papers. Until they serve you, the court has no jurisdiction. By hiding your location, you make all of this more difficult and buy time. The more difficult you make it, the more expensive it is, and eventually your adversary could cut his or her losses.

Break All Paper Trails to Your Address

Once a PI knows where you live, you're at risk for physical surveillance, harassment, dumpster diving, and all manners of trouble from someone trying to get the stuff that is rightfully yours. You're also where a process server can find you. To complete this part of the equation, you will want to carefully follow the many different ways to conceal your actual address outlined in Chapter 4.

Establish Dual Citizenship

Although this move isn't in everybody's league, if it's a possibility, dual citizenship offers you expansive opportunities to place assets out of the reach of snoops here at home.

The fight against terrorism is changing the atmosphere daily, but setting up a second citizenship gives you the ability to travel and move about the world without using a United States passport with traceable records. One note: If either of your grandparents is a first-generation Irish or Greek immigrant, you're eligible for EEU citizenship, which is a good thing.

Since Frank was going to be moving out of his common-law condo with Trixie to live with his ex and his children, he couldn't move to an unknown address, and he didn't have the resources to establish dual citizenship. He had most of his personal cash parked in his spare tire and buried among the pickets of his fence. Now it was time to salvage as much of the business assets as possible before Trixie caught on.

SAFE PLACES TO REINVEST (HIDE) YOUR CASH

BECAUSE OF THE required paper trail, money placed in the following accounts can be easily discovered and traced. Therefore, do not place your recently converted cold cash into any of the following areas:

- An existing or new account for a corporation, business, or trust traceable to your name or social security number

- A new bank account under your name

- Stocks and bonds under your name

- Cashier's checks

- Savings bonds

The Account of a Trusted Relative or Friend

To use this option, you would have your mother or girlfriend open the account and list you as a signatory. The account is then attached to the social security number of the person opening the account, not yours. You're merely a signer.

An Account Under a Defunct Domestic Corporation

I don't recommend opening a new domestic corporation, but if you have a dissolved or defunct corporation, this is one way to hide your assets right under someone's nose. If you had a corporation five years ago that wasn't successful and closed, pull out your old paperwork. That old corporation still has a FEIN number. You can walk into a local bank and open a checking account because you have the FEIN number.

Your wife and everyone think it's a dead business entity. Everyone fails to look for it. The secretary of state's database shows it's inactive and dissolved. Snoops are going to be looking for new entities, not the old dead stuff. If an investigator asks a spouse about it, your mate will reply, "Oh, that's nothing. That failed years ago."

When the terrible Trixie met him, Frank's own attempt at a business, Frank's Electrical Service, had gone under and he was working for someone else. That was part of her seduction, setting Frank up in his own business again. She knew all about his failed business. When Frank began planning to leave her, we advised him to slip some money into a new account he opened using the FEIN number of his defunct business.

An Offshore Bank Account

As in the case of my client who married the belly dancer, one good choice is to move a good portion of your money offshore. By going offshore, you entangle assets in jurisdictional issues that are too difficult and expensive to keep the dogs nipping at your heels. Furthermore, some countries won't recognize the United States government's rights to information about client's accounts.

So, to what country do you send your money? The Bahamas are no longer good. Threatened with trade restraints, they folded to the IRS. The Cayman Islands, however, told the United States government to go to hell since most of their economy is based on confidential banking. Belize and Panama are still good options. However, Guernsey, a little island off the west coast of England, is best.

You either need to travel there yourself or hire a lawyer there. You wire the money to a law firm there that opens the interest-bearing account and acts as your agent in that country.

Because you've sent funds to an attorney, your assets are now under the protection of confidentiality laws and lawyer-client privilege. Through subpoenas, your adversary can trace wire transfers. However, even though a pursuer can find out how much cash you sent to what lawyer in what country, there is no way to obtain the name of the financial shelter where the money is actually stored in that country.

Even when the belly dancer's lawyers eventually traced my client's wire transfers to the island of Guernsey, she gave up. Faced in court with the wire transfers, my client claimed he gave the money to his lawyer in Guernsey to make investments. The judge could see what had happened, but recovery was going to be problematic, if not impossible. The belly dancer called off her dogs, and my guy kept his money, even though his pride was bankrupt.

You may want to consider placing your cash in another country. With the advent of the Internet, placing money in these accounts and having access to your money is a piece of cake.

Offshore Internet Gold

If Jessie James had a laptop, he would have probably used this ultimate money shelter. As we know, the basis for all value down through history has been gold. Now, you can have some too. In a small island nation called Nevis, there exists a little-known system of creating a wall of privacy and still having ready access to your funds for paying bills, or buying what you need. The firm is known as E-Gold and their web address is www.e-gold.com.

They are not a bank, but a type of trust, and do not back your money in any currency but with real gold bullion. You can set up your own account online in five minutes or less. They have very strict secrecy laws in Nevis, and no agreement with government snoops. They will convert your gold to any currency you choose for payment and there is never a charge back. So whether it's a trust or E-Gold account you choose, you may want to take a closer look at this little island haven in the West Indies. E-Gold can be used for:

- E-commerce

- Point-of-service sales

- Person-to-person payments

- Payroll

- Bill payments

- Donations

Since E-Gold is not a bank, it does not fall under the banking laws and offers some great advantages for privacy. You can also go a step further and create an offshore trust in Nevis (See page 187). For more information on Nevis, go to www.cyberhaven.com/offshore/sample/ nevisasuperioras.html.

Accessing Money in Foreign Accounts

Once the money is offshore, accessing it is relatively easy. The money in my client's Guernsey account was easily accessed through credit cards and ATM cards.

ONLINE FOREIGN BANKING WITH ANONYMIZER. With special technology, you don't ever have to get on a plane. You can sit on your ass in the United States and conduct your banking via offshore accounts online. However, be sure to cover yourself. Use Anonymizer (www.anonymizer.com), a free website, to conduct anonymous web surfing and to link to your bank in Geneva. The website acts as a block; anyone following your trail will hit a dead end at the Anonymizer server. This program prevents anyone on the Internet from seeing your search strings or putting cookies in your hard drive. If someone does log on to your hard drive, the snoop won't know you visited the bank in the Caymans on a certain date.

Put the Cash in Prepaid Credit Cards

With no credit report required, you can place a substantial sum on a secured credit card. A good source for prepaid Visa and Mastercard information is www.rlrouse.com/prepaid-credit-cards-directory.html.

The prepaid card can also be purchased for a "friend" as a gift, and, of course, you have your friend's name put on the card. They start at amounts from $300.00 and up. You have to deposit or "pay" the cash over to the card issuer; they in turn issue a Visa card bearing your name or your friend's name, and you can charge on it until you reach the prepaid limit on the card.

This is perfectly legal, but my first experience with prepaid credit cards for assets protection was with a con man who called himself "Nick," who later ended up in jail. During my short time with Nick, he showed me the prepaid credit cards he used and told me how he enjoyed his privacy. I asked him how he obtained them and he showed me the paperwork. He had gotten the credit cards through Western

Union and he used check-cashing places to send and receive funds for mail drops and money orders.

I met Nick as a business associate of "Harry C.," a client from another state who hired me to run down a debtor, a lawyer who failed to pay Harry back a loan of $200,000, and had fled to Florida. Soon after I found the lawyer, however, I was hired by Harry C. to find Nick. Nick, it turns out, had connections in the underworld, and had bilked Harry out of $100,000 in his alleged pursuit of the deadbeat lawyer. Nick had started out small, but his demands for cash soon turned into threats to car bomb Harry's family and business.

Now Harry wanted him found, and, so far, the police had not been able to help much. Nick turned out to have multiple names, and to be a skilled con artist. I had to unravel one ID after another. In the end, I was able to locate Nick in Chicago. He was soon arrested by the FBI in the South Carolina office and spent some hard time in prison. But not for buying prepaid credit cards. I learn something from everyone.

Buy an Insurance Annuity

Plunk some bucks on an annuity with an insurance carrier unknown to the person looking for your assets. This is very difficult to trace unless your pursuer finds a record in the garbage.

Protect Your Cash with Overpayments

Another way of hiding assets is to overpay the IRS or overpay your credit cards. Later, you can file a corrected return. For the credit cards, the overpayment will simply show it as a credit on your account. You can also overpay other bills as well.

Prepayment on mortgages, in some cases, also hides available money. This is not foolproof, but very easy for someone who is examining your life to miss. You can always prepay on the principal of a mortgage and pull the money out later in an equity loan. The reverse of this would be to max out the property value in loans and hide the cash. I have seen people do this and let the property just go into foreclosure.

One person I chased did this, and is now living by the beach someplace in Mexico.

Conceal Cash with a Staged Lawsuit

This is another method for hiding cash that I've seen employed again and again over the years. You have a friend of yours sue you for the amount you want to conceal—say $20,000. You fail to show up in court and thus a judgment is entered against you for that amount. You pay your friend the $20,000 smackers, and the friend holds that money for you until after the divorce or civil court case is resolved. If a lot of money is at stake, I've seen the person staging the lawsuit put on a real show, complete with witnesses and a settlement for the actual amount the "defendant" wants the "plaintiff" to hide. Of course, you need to trust the person with whom you do this.

Even though the money surfaces, once the money's real owner is free and clear of other judgments, it's very difficult to recover, unless of course, someone can prove the staged lawsuit was actually bogus. For example, if your "friend" sued you for claiming to have hurt himself on your boat dock, but he has no medical records, witnesses, or photos to back up the claim, you may be challenged. Cover your ass here.

Conceal Cash in Collectibles

As mentioned previously, this could mean buying coins, stamps, baseball cards, sports memorabilia, antiques, or art. Some cash might go into gold coins purchased at several different coin shops or you might prefer to conceal your holdings in stamps. Both are easy to hide in some of the hiding places suggested above. These choices are seen by regular investors as hedges against inflation. Rare and expensive stamps are good cash movers; they are tiny, weigh nothing, and don't show up on any detection device. All transactions involving stamps are in cash and they can be sold/liquidated anywhere in the world on short notice.

One stamp can be worth $500,000. If anyone really diligent—like

Interpol—uncovers a cash trail, you can claim that you lost the stamp and it wasn't insured. Of course, Lloyds of London insures them every day, but they don't talk without a subpoena.

One well-known story of how creative people become when concealing assets involves a stamp and the CIA. I have heard several versions of this case, but all primarily have the same ending.

As the story goes, the CIA was after an operative from a foreign country who was scheduled to bring a huge sum of money into the United States to support their spying operations. The CIA knew who the agent was and his travel plans. They pulled his luggage, which was a small bag, and searched it thoroughly for the cash, but found nothing. They were certain he was smuggling it in. When the agent got off the plane, he entered a waiting car. Within a few blocks, another vehicle hit the operative's car, and an ambulance arrived almost immediately. According to this well-known story, the agent was placed in the ambulance, undressed, and transported to the hospital.

Meanwhile, the CIA searched his business suit and all they found was an addressed envelope in his suit jacket from a relative. The CIA was perplexed at the missing million bucks but proceeded in having their lab analyze the clothing and baggage. In the end, they found the huge amount of cash where they least expected it. The envelope in the agent's pocket, seemingly of little interest, contained a rare stamp valued at well over a million bucks. The hidden assets case was solved.

If you're thinking of protecting your hard-earned cash and your adversary is no CIA agent, you might want to think along these terms of nonobvious, hard-to-track collectibles. From baseball cards to stamps, to rare coins, comic books, antiques, paintings, and on and on. Your creative mind is the only limit. But, most of you hoping to protect your assets don't have to go to the lengths of the spy community.

CREATE AN UNTRACEABLE ASSETS SHELTER

THE BEST WAY to hide while continuing to enjoy your assets, even in the same town with the ex-spouse or ex-partner watching, is to put all of your property—vehicles, luxury toys, and business assets—in a corporation or trust that is difficult if not impossible to trace back to you. This also protects your assets and isolates your estate from creditors until you're ready to pay them.

You have a choice of several types of entities in whose name you can register your cars, boats, and property. The two most common are the corporation (the company is buying expensive condos in ski country and valuable art to go on the walls) and the trust. The key is to form a corporation or trust with a name that is not associated with you, preferably in one of the two states with strong privacy laws. If an investigator or pursuer doesn't know a trust exists, or if they guess it exists but don't know the name, you've taken a critical step toward protecting your estate from predators.

You can place your entire estate, including your primary home and everything you own—real estate, jewelry, art, vehicles, vessels, vacation homes, airplanes, business assets—in this trust or corporation. If you sell something, even your primary residence, you put the profits back in the trust. Everything recorded in property records and vehicle registrations lists the corporate name and leads back to the corporate FEIN number and, thus, its officers. In the case of a trust, the name of the trust and the officer will appear on the car or boat registration. If the trustee is your lawyer, you will begin to appreciate the attorney-client privilege rules because the investigator will have to get through him to get to you.

Form a Clandestine Domestic Trust

Although an offshore trust or corporation offers better protection, some clients prefer the domestic clandestine entity because it's easier to create a trust in this country, and somewhat easier for access.

If you've made the decision to keep your assets stateside, we then recommend securing larger assets (like real estate and vessels) and cash in a trust rather than a corporation.

Although both have to be registered with a tax ID number known to the IRS, the trust is a harder target for litigation. And if no one knows the trust exists, the untraceable name you've chosen for it, or where to look for it, you are well-protected from predators (other than the IRS, that is). Here are the best options for a domestic trust:

Form an Out-of-State Trust

I don't recommend opening a new corporation in your own state. Your name will be listed as an officer, and anyone looking for you can pull you up with a mouse click on the state's website.

NEVADA OR DELAWARE. Did you ever notice all of the trucks on the road with Nevada plates? The company could be located in Arkansas or New Jersey, but the corporation is registered in Nevada. By retaining an attorney in that state to do all of the paperwork, you can form a perfectly legal corporation or a trust. You'll be driving a Porsche registered in Delaware to MyTrust, Inc., and, because of the privacy laws in that state, if a PI runs your tag, all he'll get is the name of the corporation. That will mean nothing to him or the client. He won't know jack, and neither will the person who hired him.

You'll want to consult an attorney for the best option for your particular case, but a trust created in the states of Nevada or Delaware offers more secrecy than in the other forty-eight states due to the liberal laws in those states. The point is, you don't have to be a citizen of either state to avail yourself of the privacy laws provided by these two states. You may want to use a name that can't be associated with you or your family. You can create a trust and name it something generic, such as Security Family Trust. The only name an investigator will find on the trust is that of the registered agent—in this case, your lawyer. You and your lawyer have confidentiality. No such trust is recorded in your home state and Nevada won't release this information should an investigator get that far. It's a dead end.

You also have the option of making a relative the signatory of the trust. I have known clients to use this option to protect them if a lawyer asks, "Do you have a trust?" One client truthfully answered "no" because it was in the name of his eighteen-year-old son. The son had the trust, not him.

How a question is asked has a lot to do with whether or not the answer will be considered truthful. The question in the above example is more likely to be asked during a deposition. In depositions, lawyers have no authority to force you to say or do anything. Judges have that power. But you can't lie. That's why, when asked if he had a trust, my client's answer was correct and "truthful," because it belonged to his son.

If you set up a trust, make sure your lawyer knows about it. My client didn't tell his attorney, but called for a break to discuss his answer when he was asked the question. Just as lawyers do, you have a right to call for a break during a deposition and consult your attorney in the hallway before answering a question.

My client's ex and his lawyer suspected a trust or other asset shelter existed somewhere, but they only suspected. They couldn't prove it because they couldn't find it. And the wife's attorney didn't ask the question correctly. By putting it in his son's name, my client avoided committing perjury. No such trust was recorded in my client's home state and Nevada won't release the information. It's a dead end.

One last note: My client was very vague with his information when creating his trust. There is no law that says you must use a middle initial, although you'll find a place for it on any form you fill out. He used his son's nickname and a variation on his own on the trust documents. That brings to mind another piece of advice: Use a name untraceable to you.

At the point Frank knew he was going to leave Trixie and beg his wife to take him back, Frank followed my advice and moved some money and his assets into a trust account he opened in Nevada. His oldest son was listed as the trustee and Frank gave the trust a name that couldn't be traced to him or his family: The Eaglesmere Family Trust. Eaglesmere State Park was the place Frank and his wife had spent their honeymoon. He then moved his larger assets that he wanted to protect from Trixie's grasp into the trust: his tools, his truck, the car his wife drove, his motor boat, all things he'd brought to his marriage with Trixie.

Open an Offshore Corporation or Trust

Although an out-of-state trust is an excellent shelter, the superior protection and tax advantages to the offshore trust account should get your attention. Perhaps in the same institution where you've created an offshore bank account, you can establish a virtually untraceable haven for the big stuff.

In the process of moving his money offshore, Frank formed an offshore corporation in Guernsey. Belize and Panama are no longer good options. You either need to travel there yourself or hire a lawyer there. You wire the money to a law firm there, which establishes the corporation, makes the deposits, and acts as your agent in that country.

The beauty of this is that you can place domestic assets in the offshore corporation: real estate, including your primary residence, your BMW, your artwork, and the new backhoe you just bought.

Because you've sent funds to an attorney, your assets are now under the protection of confidentiality laws and lawyer-client privilege. Through subpoenas, your adversary can trace wire transfers. However, even though a pursuer can find out how much cash you sent and to what country, they have no way to know the money's final resting place in that country. They have your lawyer's name—the one that's not talking—but they don't know where he or she's put the money. No one who's looking for your assets knows the name of the corporation. Some people make this doubly difficult by creating a trust rather than a corporation. Certain corporations must be registered, whereas not all nations require a trust to be recorded. This is just an edge in keeping spies out of your cash accounts.

Consider Nevis

Nevis, the home of E-Gold (mentioned earlier in this chapter), has some great trust opportunities available and their laws even require any plaintiff to first deposit a $25,000 bond before any suit can be accepted for filing. Nevis will not recognize any nondomestic court orders regarding asset protection. The trust documents are not public record and not required to be filed with the government in Nevis. Again, for more information on Nevis, go to www.cyberhaven.com/offshore/sample/nevisasuperioras.html.

Frank was happy holding his cash in the truck tire and his assets in an out-of-state trust and a defunct corporation until the ink was dry on his divorce to the terrible Trixie. At the final hearing, Trixie again tried to find out what Frank had done with the cash she claimed had been in their joint accounts. Frank apologized for losing it all at the dog track.

SEVEN

THE ART OF SURVEILLANCE

LET'S SUPPOSE YOU want to follow the movements of a business partner who you think is pocketing more than his half, a husband you think is boffing your best friend, a daughter you think is on drugs, or an employee you suspect is a mole for the competition. How can you do this undetected? Throw away the wigs and the make-up kit. To make it as a do-it-yourself dick, you must master how to disguise your vehicle, to be a chameleon blending into the environment, to deflect curious onlookers with plausible reasons, to prevent having a confrontation with the law, and, of course, to avoid being made by the target. Consider the following statistics:

PERCENTAGE OF CASES THAT INVOLVE TAILING: 70

PERCENTAGE WHO CATCH A PROFESSIONAL TAILING THEM: 10

PERCENTAGE OF DIVORCE CASES THAT REQUIRE TAILING A SPOUSE: 95

NUMBER OF VEHICLES USED TO CONDUCT A ONE-WEEK TAIL: 6

NUMBER OF VEHICLES USED ON A SINGLE TAIL: 2 to 4

PERCENTAGE OF MARKS WHO ARE LOOKING FOR A TAIL: 60

PERCENTAGE OF CASES RESOLVED WITH EVIDENCE FROM TAILING: 90 to 95

CHANCES THAT TAILING IS ILLEGAL IF YOU HAVE A LEGITIMATE LEGAL REASON: 0

COST PER HOUR TO HIRE A TOP PI TO CONDUCT SURVEILLANCE: $75

COST TO HIRE YOURSELF: 0 to $350

Surveillance—whether electronic or by car, on foot, or in a fixed position—is an essential skill for any amateur PI. Over 70 percent of my cases—from fidelity cases to landlord disputes—involve surveillance, and a high percentage of the evidence used in most civil cases derives from shadowing a target. I've tailed ex-wives to prove they have a live-in lover; because of a cohabitation clause in the divorce, my clients stand to reduce alimony or improve their custody rights if mommy has moved a boy toy into the household. I've represented employers who want more information about the lifestyle of an employee they are planning to hire or promote. Recently, the majority of those targets have been teenagers, and that usually means drugs are involved. When parents hire me to tail their teenager, it's because they don't want little Johnny involved with the police. Better to find the dealer themselves and call the cops on the jerk who's selling to their kid than risk having their kid busted.

In this chapter, you'll learn how to employ the kind of cover that has worked for the pros. In the twenty-two years I've spent tailing hundreds of spouses, teenagers, employers, employees, coworkers, girlfriends, mistresses, fiancés, lovers, neighbors, and people at the other end of a legal dispute, I've perfected tactics that have enabled me and other private investigators to tail a mark undetected for hours and days. In one of my more satisfying cases, I followed the cheating husband of a broken-hearted relative to help her during a divorce. After changing my age range, and adding a scar to my face and a sag to my shoulders, I came within seven feet of the low-life, philandering scum, and the yo-yo never knew it was me. To this day, he doesn't know I snapped the pictures that turned his ass to toast in court.

In this chapter, I've distilled these tricks into some simple suggestions that mean the difference between losing a tail or staying with one. You'll learn how to tail a mark by foot, by car, and in a fixed position, and you will also learn how to sanitize your vehicle so it won't be recognized when you spend miles behind the mark's rearview mirror. You'll learn lane and traffic positions. You also need to look like a person who's a chameleon in any surroundings. The chapter will give you a list of what props to have with you. Your props and cover story also depend in part on whether you're in your car or on foot. It is often the subtle things that will blow your cover and small details are of the utmost importance. In this chapter, we will also cover some techniques used for electronic surveillance, at least those that can be employed legally. For example, audiotaping without the knowledge of the mark is illegal in just about every instance. However, you can perform video surveillance as long as the audio is turned off. Today's video cameras are so small they can be hidden just about anywhere. The most well-known use of such devices are the "nanny cams" concerned parents have used in the recent years to determine if their children are being abused.

But physical surveillance is also often the first step, even if it doesn't solve the case. For example, a Latin businessman suspected that his wife was having an affair. He engaged us to identify his wife's lover, establish the seriousness of the relationship, and gather the ammunition needed to confront her and expose her gigolo lover, even though he had no intention of divorcing her.

His wife had had affairs before and was what we refer to in the business as a "hard target." We started tailing her at 7:00 a.m. and stayed with her all day until she went to bed at midnight. We had to use two tail cars and work in two shifts to cover the entire day. On day three, we had to totally change the color, make, and models of the vehicles being used. She never made us, but we also never made her and the lover. We never caught her meeting a man or in some parking lot with the lover. We tailed her all over town. We followed her to the gym for her workout, her tennis lessons, her friend's house on a nearby location, and even grocery shopping. We were able to stay with her an entire week without her realizing we were there and recorded several hours of videotape detailing her movements.

One of the strange occurrences we observed during this case was that, even though this target had a cell phone and home phones, she went to the nearest drugstore two blocks away and used the pay phone to make calls. Not only did she use it to make phone calls, but on several occasions she sat on the bench next to the phone with a book waiting until the phone rang. Bingo.

When we reported this to our client, we asked him to recover the cell phone bills for the last three months so we could examine the calls. She made one call continuously, always for just one minute. She was clearly arranging for the lover to call her on the pay phone. We were able to identify the name of the subject based on repeat phone calls and when we mentioned the name to the client, he knew it as her personal trainer, a buffed airhead who was clearly doing more than building up the quads of his trophy wife.

Not only did our client know the man, but he had also trained with Mr. Muscles during which he had often bragged about his escapades with rich, married women. Deeper research on the cell phone showed that the times she was calling the personal trainer were inappropriate, such as one at 3:00 on a Friday morning. It wasn't rocket science to assume our client's young wife was looking for a sex machine, not a Nautilus machine, at that hour.

Although we got electronic clues later to help us actually identify the lover, we had to begin with physical surveillance. And this is a skill you need, too, if you're going to play PI.

In the end, there is no perfect way to conduct surveillance. Even the FBI loses its targets. Your brain is your most important piece of equipment. The way you analyze, calculate, and plan will have a significant effect on the outcome of your case.

PREPARATION AND PLANNING

JUST WHEN YOU'RE confident that your cheating rat spouse or loser teen isn't expecting you on their tail, they see you rounding a corner. You need to behave like a pro so you don't have to hire one after you've blown your cover. That means plan, strategize, and prepare. So much of successful tailing does not occur during the actual car chase. It's pure preparation.

It's just too easy to get spotted. Even the professionals get made by a wary mark. Once I was hired by the wife of another PI. He and I were busy outsmarting each other. One night, he suddenly pulled up to a bar. I did too, then waited in the parking lot for him to come back out. However, I didn't realize that he had walked out the back door until he came up behind me, stuck a gun to my head and said "You want something, motherfucker?" I said, "No, I'm just waiting for my sister."

Surveillance can be compared to a live human chess game. Sometimes you have to plan your strategy two or three moves in advance, and sometimes you have to make a particular move to cause an opponent to react in a certain way. Here are some of the typical steps professionals follow while planning surveillance, steps you need to take if you want to play PI.

Select the Most Logical Mode for Surveillance

Every case is different. Depending on the target and the route, you can conduct surveillance by car, bicycle, on foot, or a combination of these. A car should be your first choice. Make sure it has plenty of zip, but a plain-jane model. If gated communities will be involved, a folding bicycle in the trunk can help get in where other vehicles cannot.

Shadowing a Mark from the Same Address

If your mark is your spouse or child, I don't recommend that you follow them from home. In fact, I don't recommend it even if the mark lives at a different address. Normally, I don't have my operatives tail a mark from the mark's home. A suspicious target who is up to no good starts checking his or her rearview mirror right away. The mark is much more relaxed once he has assured himself that no one has left behind him from the same street.

LEAVE EARLIER. Make an early morning appointment requiring you to leave the house first. Pick up the tail along the mark's regular route.

GET THE TIME. If your spouse, child, or roommate leaves for work before you on a regular basis, you can check on his or her leaving time with a simple trick. Buy a cheap watch with sweep hands on it; they can be found for as little as five bucks. Remove the band and use a marker to dull the case. Place this watch under the rear wheel of the person's car, and when the mark drives away the car tire will crush the hands in place, telling you for sure what time he or she left. If the person usually leaves before you wake up, this will be helpful in establishing surveillance times and tactics. If the mark has to be at work at 7:00 a.m. and the watch shows the rat is leaving the ship at 5:00 a.m., you might want to find out what the person living with you is doing with the two hours before work. There's more here than a donut with coffee.

SET UP THE MARK. If you share the same address, send the person you're going to follow on a goose chase with a real or bogus errand on the way to work. Select a specific drugstore or business from where you can pick up the trail, either by car or on foot. This gives you a chance to get your covert vehicle moving without the mark seeing you follow him or her directly from home.

PICK UP THE TAIL FROM AN APPOINTMENT. Check date books, calendars, and address books. Plan to begin the tail from one of the mark's planned destinations, such as a dentist appointment or business luncheon.

PICK UP THE TAIL ALONG A REGULAR ROUTE OR LOCATION. Falling in behind the mark on his or her routine drive to school or work will be a more natural occurrence, as other traffic will be joining the roadway. A target seldom suspects the car that pulls out of the burger joint a mile into his trip. Based on research or personal knowledge of the mark's schedule, follow a teenager from the bus stop or a friend's house; a spouse from work, the gym, or an appointment; a coworker from the office; and a legal rival from that person's workplace. You get the picture.

Shadowing a Mark with Whom You Don't Live

Again, although each case is different, I don't recommend that you shadow a mark from their home, where they are most likely to be on alert. Plan to follow them from school, work, the gym, a restaurant, or some other public place they will be if at all possible. Follow these steps as part of your preparation.

Study the Mark's Vehicle

When conducting any surveillance, you want to make sure you're thoroughly familiar with the vehicle that your target will be driving. When night surveillance is possible, I've known agents who have used an ice pick to put a small hole in the taillight of the target's vehicle. This small hole will then stand out like a bright beacon among the other taillights if you happen to be following them in heavy traffic or down congested roadways. This clearly helps you to identify the vehicle even if it's an extended distance in front of you.

Conduct a Field Review of the Route

While you know the mark is at work, school, or out of town, you may want to take the actual route your mate, teenager, or sleazy business partner follows. Or is likely to follow. You'll need to predict the route of travel that your target may take. If he or she is coming from work, try to find the most convenient way from point A to point B that avoids most of the traffic and saves the most amount of time because this is exactly what your target is likely to do. Remember, I said "likely" because there are no guarantees in this business.

Become thoroughly familiar with the route you're going to be traveling, and you'll know if you're going to be encountering one-way streets or bottlenecks in your path. This will allow you to be more prepared when you actually shadow the loser.

In your field review, also predict where else your spouse or teenager might stop on the way to a location such as work or school. It could be that your spouse is a coffee drinker and frequently stops at a fast-food chain. If you identify those locations, it will help you in advance to predict his habits and patterns.

The field review is especially valuable because you'll be alert to moves that don't make sense. If your spouse is driving from home to work and varies in a direction that is totally out of the way to the office, it will give you a pretty good idea that he's not headed to work.

Case the Fixed Surveillance Location

One of the first things that you'll want to do is drive by the fixed surveillance location. This may be your spouse's workplace or it may be a suspected girlfriend's or boyfriend's house. As you're driving through the section of town, you'll want to look for a surveillance point where your vehicle is going to blend in. Your car or van needs to look like a vehicle that belongs where it's going to be for the length of time that it may be there. This tells you which car to drive and how to disguise or prepare a vehicle for a stakeout.

SELECT PRIMARY AND SECONDARY SURVEILLANCE POINTS. This can be as simple as driving around the neighborhood of the suspected girlfriend's or boyfriend's house assessing the best vantage point for watching the front door. You'll also want to find yourself a fall-back position because if something goes wrong or someone gets too nosy at your primary surveillance spot, you need to have a second place you can pull back to and still have a window of visibility to your target.

Qualities of a Good Surveillance Vehicle

Most surveillance today is done by car, van, or motorcycle. The vehicle can be your best friend and an excellent tool or it can give you away from the very beginning. The first thing you need to do is assess the type of vehicle that you're going to use. Even though TV investigators drive their red Ferraris, Porsches, or muscle cars, real PIs always choose a vehicle that is a plain jane. Maybe you don't have a nondescript car or a car that can be disguised well. Each case is different. You don't want the target to recognize the vehicle. That's the bottom line. If possible, the vehicle you use for surveillance should be unknown to the target and it should have no identifying characteristics—in other words, a Plain Jane. This can be borrowed from a friend or rented; this choice, however, could compromise your secrecy or cost you bucks.

The Plain Jane

If you're going to rent or borrow a car, choose a car with nondescript characteristics. It should be a family style vehicle, perhaps a four-door sedan, and the color should be generic. Gray is generally the best color for any type of surveillance work since it's a neutral color. So if you have a choice, a plain jane is recommended.

Whether you're using your own car, a borrowed car, or a rental, make sure there are no distinctive features that could jump out at your target if you shadow your mark more than once. Make sure there aren't any dents; no oversized antennae; no car rack; and certainly no ornaments, stickers, or decals. Make sure there isn't anything on the vehicle that will distinguish it from any other vehicle of the same make and model on the roadway. Regardless of whether the mark knows the car, be sure you've removed any distinctive items that could be recognized when you pull in behind the mark the next day. These include:

- **Bumper stickers**

- **Windshield or window decals**

- **Front custom license plate (not a legal plate; a private citizen would be violating the law by removing a legal license plate)**

Engine Power

Whichever vehicle you use should be equipped with an engine that has enough power to do short bursts of speed during the surveillance. There will be many times when you will have to back off and then close up the gap between yourself and your target.

Confirm the Car Is in Working Order

You will want to make sure the vehicle is in good working order. Remember when you start a vehicle surveillance you could travel anywhere from one mile to 1,000 miles, depending on the circumstances, so make sure you:

- **Check air in the tires**

- **Check all of the fluids in the vehicle**

- **Check if the driver's sun visor is working (you'll need it)**

- **Check the parking-light lenses and light system. Go out after dark and turn on the headlights and taillights of the vehicle you are going to use. Walk down in front of the vehicle approximately 100 feet and look back at the** adjustment of the headlights and make sure they are adjusted equally, and that there are no parking lights or marker lights burned out. These would be a dead give-away during a surveillance.

- Make sure the vehicle has rearview and side mirrors. Many times I've conducted surveillance by pointing the vehicle in the opposite direction of the target and actually observing the targets through the rearview mirrors while pointed away from them.

Prepare Your Pretexts or Excuses

When you're in a strange environment, either following a person down a street or sitting in a car conducting a stakeout, never reveal the true reason you're there. When some bystander, neighbor, or cop asks, "What are you doing here?" be ready with a plausible explanation.

Remember, people love to help kids and pets. Everyone can relate to that. Otherwise, ask yourself, "Who would have a right to be here at this location, doing a thing that's natural for this area, at this time of day?"

I once used an artist's easel and set up on a beach. I can't even draw stick men, but apparently, my random spatterings of paint on the canvas was pretty impressive to some passersby. They called it abstract art and one person even told me she saw the universe and the ocean's power in my splashed paint. What I was actually doing was running a video camera in the brown paper bag on the ground. I was videotaping a second-floor condo and the couple making out on the lanai. I have been a telephone man, a survey taker, a traffic counter, a nuisance wildlife trapper, and a host of other personas.

As you develop your pretext, you will also be collecting stakeout props to support it. Here are some suggestions:

Missing Children's Help Foundation Pretext

Produce a missing-child card from your own mail, the ones that are frequently sent to all mailboxes in a certain neighborhood. Pretext: "I'm in your neighborhood because there's a report that this child may have been sighted here. I'm with the Missing Children's Help Foundation. I'm going to park here for an hour or two to see if I see the child or the vehicle. Can I give you a copy? If you see the child, please call this number." Giving a number always dispels anxiety. I always give the number (860)525-7078, a bogus number that always rings busy because it is a test line for the phone company (they have three that I know of).

Lost Pet Pretext

Place a leash and dog biscuits on the seat next to you, then produce a picture of a dog, maybe a poster or flyers of it. Pretext: "Have you seen this dog? Someone said they saw it in this neighborhood. My daughter took the call. Hopefully the dog will appear." Explain that your kids will kill you if you don't recover the dog. Now everybody knows why you are up and down the street all day, sitting and watching for a few hours at a time.

American Traffic Foundation Pretext

Here's where you need a hard hat and clipboard. Say you're with the American Traffic Foundation. Your job is to track the flow of traffic on city streets between hours of x and x. Again, give the curious one of the phony 800 numbers. You may even want to hand them a traffic survey form you made on your home computer to "mail in."

Real Estate Photography Pretext

This pretext explains the existence of the camera or video camera and the actual taking of pictures. Say you've been hired to photograph homes and neighborhoods for:

- A real estate company, and you're waiting for a Realtor to meet you there

- Comps for a real estate appraisal

- Your insurance company for homeowner's insurance (Some companies even have my agency do that.)

- A *Lands and Homes* magazine feature article on this area of town

Old Neighborhood Pretext

This is a good excuse if you're caught without any props. Pretext: "I'm waiting for my sister from Louisiana. I used to live here, and she only knows how to find this address. She's driving in from New York. I hope she's going to be in anytime soon."

Disguise the Vehicle

If you're using your own car, remove any recognizable objects, decals, stickers, etc. I've known clients to borrow a license plate for the day. You might want to add some different bumper stickers. If you have a bumper sticker already on the car, remove it so it won't be recognizable.

Whether you're using your car, a borrowed car, or a rental, you can disguise the car further for moving or fixed surveillance with props that match up to one or more of the pretexts you're prepared to employ during the stakeout.

Magnetic Signs

A removable magnetic sign can be added to a car to bolster a pretext and disguise the vehicle. These can be ordered from any local sign shop for $30. You can have more than one to change the car's appearance during the course of the day's or week's surveillance. Make up possible names.

You may want a gender-specific business sign, especially if the mark you're following knows you. A female can change the appearance of a car with a sign that suggests a male driver. These magnetic signs are handy and can be slapped on the side of your car when on fixed surveillance in order to dispel any suspicions or to set up a believable pretext. If a nosy neighbor approaches while you're staking out a house, your story that you're a realtor waiting to meet a client will appear more believable if you have a fictitious "Century Homes Real Estate" magnetic sign hanging on the side of your car.

ADD ITEMS TO THE DASHBOARD. Sales brochures and tape measures can make the car look like a work vehicle and make it consistent with any sign you may be using.

BUSINESS CARDS. You can further promote this alternate identity by actually having a matching card from the company you're allegedly representing. The business cards to match the signs can be readily made up in small quantity at your local office-supply store.

Bring a Sunshade
This can be propped up in the windshield of your car. Make a small hole, large enough to peer through, or to actually take hidden photographs or video recordings.

Disguise the Driver
A simple disguise using a baseball hat and sunglasses will keep you from being identified as a female. Tuck your hair up under the cap. If you don't wear them, use eyeglasses. Old sunglasses or old glasses with the lenses out will look like prescription glasses. A contrasting-color shirt to change into during the tail will help the mark from making you.

Although tinted windows are an advantage, put down the sunshades to disguise portions of your face while driving if your windows aren't tinted.

Gather Essential Surveillance Equipment

What follows is a list of the basic items you'll need for surveillance. For more specific information on these items, see Appendix 2 on page 263.

Binoculars

A set of binoculars is essential. They don't have to be real expensive, either. One of the best ways to conceal yourself as you're doing the surveillance is to keep some distance between you and your target. Remember that there is an immediate awareness zone and the closer that you get to a target, the more likely you are to be noticed or even identified. If you do get identified, your job will be a thousand times harder in all respects. The best type of binoculars to use in this case would be small with at least an 8x magnification. One such set of affordable binoculars can be purchased at your local department store for about $25. They are small enough to be easily concealed in a jacket pocket should someone approach your vehicle. If you have a few extra bucks to spend, you can even buy a pair with a built-in digital camera. These binoculars normally can be found at Radio Shack in the price range of $60 to $80.

Camera

A high-tech camera is great, but a simple, easy-to-use one will do. I caught one cheating husband and his morning jumpstart with an instamatic camera built into a Pepsi can. A 110-film camera fits perfectly in a pop can. You can stick your finger in the hole and push the button. You want to be sure to do a test run on your camera and make sure that it's operating and capturing good images. You'll want to make sure that no giveaway red lights or flashes of any nature go off during your filming or photographing. Make sure that you not only have fresh batteries in your unit but that you have an extra battery that you can carry with you as well. If you have a backup camera, that's even better.

Video Camera

This is essential spyware these days, but it doesn't have to be top of the line. If you can afford it, a palm-sized digital video camera would be best. Next would be a small 8mm camcorder, and last would be a VHS camcorder, but these are larger and more likely to draw attention. You can go the James Bond route, however. There's a video camera the size of a quarter you can wear on a necktie. A fellow detective used one of these to get live footage of a deep kissing session between a mark and his lover in a dimly lit cocktail lounge. The cheater went to the cleaners and his wife got the house. These types of video cameras can also be used for hidden electronic surveillance, which I discuss later in this chapter.

Microcassette Tape Recorder

This can be obtained for as little as $25 at most major department stores. This will become handy because, as you conduct your surveillance, you will need to make as many notes as possible. You'll need to document dates, times, color of clothing, addresses, vehicle descriptions, and a host of other details as you close in on your prey. Make sure that during your surveillance you also have a notepad and a pen.

Hearing Amplifier

This device amplifies sound twenty times; it looks like a transistor radio that can be carried in shirt pocket, with an earplug. At $25, it is sold for use at concerts and sporting events to better hear announcers and performers. This bad boy will hear a whisper at thirty feet. This is also very bad news, however, if someone blows a car horn in your ear.

GPS Cell Phone

You should have a regular cell phone at a minimum. However, GPS phones are becoming more affordable, so in planning your tactics you may want to incorporate the use of some type of a GPS device in order to help track your child or spouse, especially if you're new at surveillance or find that your driving is not aggressive enough to stay up with your target's driving habits. I mentioned how to use GPS devices in Chapter 1, so go to page 20 for review.

Personal Supplies

Since a vehicle tail combined with a stakeout may take hours through different times of day and weather, be prepared with:

- Full tank of gas

- Food and water

- Personal medications

- A watch

- Appropriate changes of clothes for weather and time of day. If you're working in a cold part of the country, you'll want to be sure that you have ample warm clothing because you will not be able to continually idle your car without being noticed.

Do not bring a gun! Forget that .45-caliber Colt; you'll have no need for that in this business and it will only get you in trouble.

And forget entertainment. Although surveillance can be very boring and tedious, do not bring a magazine, portable television or anything else that is going to distract your attention away from observing your target. I cannot tell you how many times I've seen an investigator glance at a newspaper or magazine only to look up thirty seconds later and find out his or her target has left the location without his knowledge.

SHADOWING THE MARK BY CAR

NOW YOU'RE READY to actually begin the tail. As you can see, it wasn't as easy as jumping over the back of your convertible and sailing down the road, watching for the mark from behind your shades. Most surveillance work is in the preparation.

Get Ready to Move

Whether you're pulling out from a side street or commercial parking lot to pick up your tail from a bogus errand or a dentist appointment, you'll want to observe the following tactics:

- Park 100 feet away or more.

- In a neighborhood, park at another lot line because neighbor A will think someone must be visiting my neighbor and neighbor B will think the same.

- In a commercial setting, park to blend in.

- Using the pretext of looking at a map or reading the paper, wait for the mark to complete the bogus errand and start his car.

- Start your car.

- Sit patiently until a car is between you and your mark and then pull out two car lengths behind, heading in the same direction.

Tailing Tactics

From your vantage point of two car lengths back, grit your teeth as your mark drives right past the gym where they claimed to be working out every morning. So where is the bastard going? You have to follow to find out. Here are some basic tactics for tailing with a car:

- Two-lane road: Remain at least two car lengths behind.

- Four-lane road: Travel in the lane beside the target, either right or left, but not behind them. Ninety percent of drivers who are suspicious of being followed or feeling guilty about their destination will check the center rear-view mirror as opposed to the side mirrors. They are generally concerned with the car immediately to their rear.

- Approaching an intersection: Change lanes to move temporarily behind the mark in case they decide to make a turn. If the target doesn't turn, move back to the side lane.

- Congested traffic: Remain two car lengths behind in the side lane.

- Thinning traffic patterns: Drop back three or four lengths.

- Dead end: If the mark turns down a dead-end street, do not follow them! If your target made a wrong turn, he or she will most certainly see you on the way out, as you were traveling in. If it turns out that your target doesn't come back, the mystery destination may be down that street. You'll know it soon enough when the mark's car doesn't come back out.

When to Turn Tail

Knowing when to pull off is another important aspect of surveillance. If you see your mark making u-turns on a four-lane road, you're going to have to make a choice; if you make the same u-turn, he or she's most likely going to identify you as a tail car. You may very well have to decide to let him go and come back another day. This is an example of the types of judgment calls only you can make in the field, depending on the circumstances. If you're following your tail and he or she continues to make circling turns or circles in a parking lot, be very wary; he may be on to you. If so, it's time to turn tail and retreat.

Be Prepared to Make Stops

Adapt your tactics to the mark's destination. Your target could be going to any one of a variety of places, so adjust your next step accordingly. Your spouse will meet the lover—or your teenager a drug dealer—in a residential, commercial, or rural setting, each of which offers separate fixed surveillance requirements.

Residential Setting Stop

If the mark pulls into a driveway or parks on the street in a residential neighborhood, continue driving past him or her. Turn in the first driveway and return, heading the opposite direction, and:

- Park where there is a window of visibility.

- Straddle the lot line between two properties.

- Head in the opposite direction from the target and view his or her movements through the rearview mirror.

- Park at least 300 feet away and to the side of the road, simulating an auto breakdown by raising the hood in a rural neighborhood.

- Use binoculars.

- If approached by some nosy neighbors or Good Samaritans offering to help you with your broken car, tell them your brother is on the way, or that you've already called a tow truck. Or, you can use one of the pretexts mentioned previously in this chapter.

- Write down the license plate numbers of any cars in the driveway or parked on the street.

- Take down the address and other information about this destination. Even if you don't see your spouse actually embrace another person, an employee accept a bribe from a corporate spy, or your child accept a baggie of coke from a sleazeball, you have the address of someone you didn't know existed. Someone who holds the key to where your target does something he or she doesn't want you to know about. We discovered that the husband of one of my clients had bought himself a Jaguar when we ran the license plates on the street near the apartment of his mistress. His wife had no idea about the purchase.

- Observe the target's exit. Is the target with someone at the door? Do you know the person? Is there someone watching from the door, waving goodbye, or discreetly pulling aside a curtain?

Commercial Setting Stop

- Park to blend in.

- Use the pretext of looking at a map or reading the paper.

- Observe the entrance. Note any single customers who enter soon after your mark. If you don't know the identity of the lover, corporate mole, or drug dealer, watch for a customer entering alone who seems in a hurry and looking for someone.

- Be cool. If you recognize the person meeting your mark, don't blow your cover by jumping out of your car and confronting the lover or drug dealer.

- Wait for your mark to leave and observe him or her. Were they meeting someone? Notice if someone alone leaves soon after. Is the target carrying anything? How long does the target stay?

- Write down and/or tape-record the address and details of the setting.

Shift Focus to the Other Person

If you don't know the mysterious person your husband, employee, or daughter met at the bistro for lunch, drop the original target, and follow the mystery person. Follow him or her to a place of work or a residential address and get tag numbers, addresses, and details. If it's a lover, perhaps you'll surprise him or her at a meeting; if it's a corporate spy, you'll find out where the sleazebag works.

Now that you have an address and the license plate numbers of the cars in the driveway or on the street in front of the house where your spouse spent a secret hour or your teenager appears to have scored dope, you're ready to find out the identity of the mystery lover, dealer, or loan shark. You can do this now by reviewing the tactics outlined in Chapter 3 and Chapter 5.

SHADOWING THE MARK ON FOOT

THERE WILL BE times when you will find it necessary to shadow the mark on foot. To do that, you'll need some special equipment, and will have to change your tactics. Some special equipment you'll need:

- Spy glasses. For about $8, you can buy sunglasses that have a mirrored inner surface. You can see where you're going, but also what's behind you. These actually are marketed as "spy glasses."

- Small binoculars in pocket or monocular size (a single-tube monocular is about $20).

- A small hand mirror. If the mark stops, another trick is to carry a small hand mirror and stand with your back to the mark and observe him or her in the mirror.

- Sunglasses and a hat if tailing in daylight.

- Comfortable shoes that make very little noise (No hard heels that clack on the street.)

- Props to ensure that you look like you belong in the environment you're tailing in. Such items would be: shopping bags, a clipboard, a dog leash, or a missing animal poster and hammer.

Personal Disguise

Only you know how far you have to go to hide your identity if surveilling on foot. Hiding behind a tree and jungle camouflage aren't options, however. If the mark knows you, you have to choose between actually disguising yourself or staying at an extreme distance and increasing the chances of losing the target. To help change your personal appearance:

- Visit the costume shop. You can find appearance aids such as scar wax, wigs, and facial hair for men or women, and props such as fake crutches and canes.

- Visit the thrift store (objects are often cheaper than renting from the costume shop) for clothes that are out of style—shoes, overcoats, and other props. But don't get too extreme as to attract attention.

- Change your age. Although I was about thirty-eight, some old wire-rim glasses, a cane, a gray wig, and some padding stuffed around my waist bumped me up twenty years into "old guy." I completed my transformation with old-man baggy pants and wingtip shoes from a 1950s thrift shop.

- Change your walk and adapt your appearance. Don't try to limp, but walk more slowly or more quickly. I slumped over while walking, using the cane. Try to fit in by wearing clothes appropriate for the area.

Paralleling

Depending on the amount of foot traffic and the area you are in, it is sometimes better to follow a mark by walking on the opposite side of the street and in the same direction he or she is going. In the biz, we call this paralleling. Anyone who suspects he or she is being followed usually looks right behind them.

Watch the Window

Many times you can also watch the mark by seeing his or her reflection in glass storefronts.

Blend In

Remember to blend in as much as possible. Stay with a group of pedestrians as opposed to always being the lone wolf. Be sure to dress in the mode that most of the people will be wearing in that area. You'd look out of place in a three-piece suit walking through an industrial zone. On the other hand, faded torn Levi's and a tank top would be out of place following someone through the New York Stock Exchange.

Change Clothes

Removing a black jacket and wearing a white shirt or other color sometimes helps to confuse the mark as to whether you're the same person he or she noticed before.

Appear Occupied

If the mark stops, you stop and look in a window. Occupy yourself. You can also duck into doorways or stores.

CONDUCTING A STAKEOUT

IN THE PI business, a stakeout is known as "fixed surveillance." In this instance, you will observe the mark from a single, fixed location.

Conduct an intelligent, well-planned stakeout. Be prepared using the steps outlined above, as well as the ones listed below:

- Complete a field review and select your post.

- Disguise the vehicle or yourself if you're on foot.

- Select your pretexts.

- Bring the proper props to support your pretexts.

- Have adequate supplies.

- Park with visibility, but on a property line.

- Develop a relationship with a neighbor down the street, a comrade in an area your target visits. That will save you a lot of time. This is someone you can ask, "Was that car in the driveway again?" There's no substitute for help from a local. Especially if it's a protracted battle in which you wish to successfully complete many undetected stakeouts.

- Read the newspaper with your fake glasses if you're conducting your spying from a park bench. You won't have your face on display, and the paper provides a shield for camera work. You might cut a hole in the newspaper.

Collect Evidence that Will Hold Up in Court

Read Appendix One on how to legally collect evidence and secure it properly. In addition, follow these steps:

- Log exact times and dates. This may just be the mark's movements, destinations, and contacts. If you're a witness to events, your log will stand as proof that an employee met with the competition or that a salesman is not fulfilling his or her route and meeting customers. This may be what your lawyer needs to prove that the bastard who said he was going to work was really working out position number 144 with his girlfriend.

■ **Find witnesses to subpoena.** Document tag numbers of persons in the area who could be witnesses to events you've seen. Identify the witnesses in your log or in the video and photos who appear to be interacting with or watching the mark.

■ **Look for additional coverage.** Search the surroundings for security cameras mounted on businesses and recover copies of tapes to shore up your own evidence.

■ **The watch trick.** To identify how long a person has stayed at a location, buy a cheap wristwatch and perform the same time-check-under-the-tires trick suggested earlier on page 194 to gauge the time a person leaves the house.

■ **Carry an empty paper bag** with camera, film, and batteries. Tear a hole in the bag for the camera lens. Snap the picture while appearing to be holding up the paper bag or rummaging through it. Fancy camera work will come in handy here, as well as some technology. One useful piece of spyware is an attachment to the camera lens with a mirror that allows you to photograph what's to the side instead of what you're aiming at.

■ **Use a small tape recorder** to keep track of your photographic record. As you take a picture, speak into the recorder giving date, time, and view, so it will match up to the negatives. For example, "Number one: This is the east view of Susan Brown's house from approximately 100 feet away."

ELECTRONIC VIDEO SURVEILLANCE: NANNY CAMS AND HIDDEN CAMERAS

TODAY, THERE ARE literally cameras on every street corner, cameras on the freeways, at intersections, inside sports arenas, almost every place you go. Video technology has changed rapidly in the last five years, and it is now used for surveillance more than in any other area. Known as Nanny Cams, these tiny cameras, some as small as a dime, can be hidden into devices as small as a ballpoint pen. And, the prices have fallen to the point where you can set up a wireless spy-camera system for less than $300, in about thirty minutes.

Before purchasing a hidden camera, there's a few things you need to know. There's a lot of equipment available, but not all of it is good. One of the most disappointing things that can happen is when you purchase a video unit that advertises the ability to send a wireless signal up to 100 yards, only to find out that it will only send a signal across the room. Worse yet, you end up with one of the systems that has so much "drift" that it will not stay on frequency, and the picture only comes in and out once every ten minutes. This guide will help you avoid some of the pitfalls and give you a few tips on employing and using hidden video.

VIDEO CAMERA BASICS

WIRELESS VIDEO SYSTEMS work just like TV stations that broadcast in your area. Basically, the components consist of a miniature video camera with a transmitter. The video camera picks up the image, transfers it via radio wave over a specific distance, where it is then received by a receiver, much like your own TV set. The receiver then converts the signal back into a video image once again and displays it on your monitor or sends it to your recording device. To sum it up, the components are: a camera, a transmitter, a receiver, a recorder, or a monitor device for viewing the video. Almost all tiny cams today have the transmitter built inside the unit.

Multiple Cameras

In some cases, you may want to employ more than one camera on a single job. If you're going to have two or more cameras, then a third component must be added, which is commonly referred to as a "switcher." All a switcher does is switch back and forth between camera one and camera two at predetermined time intervals, such as five seconds, and it actually enables you to record from two cameras at the same time.

Power Output and Frequency

One of the most important considerations when using wireless hidden video is the transmit power output. If you are purchasing a wireless video camera, one of the first questions you need to ask is how many milliwatts of power the unit transmits. I've seen hidden wireless video cameras for sale with as little as 200 milliwatts output. I've also seen hidden video cameras for sale with as high as 1 watt output.

Be advised that if you exceed a certain limit, you will be required to get an FCC license, much like your local TV stations. For that reason, most of the wireless video systems you encounter will be less than 1 watt. I make sure that the unit that I am using has at least 800 milliwatts of transmit power. Units requiring a license will be marked as such.

The second consideration is what frequency the wireless camera transmits at. I have seen hidden wireless cameras transmit anywhere from 400 megahertz up to 2.4 gigahertz. The latter is a much higher frequency and the higher the frequency, the better penetration ability you generally have in going through walls, brush, or structure. The high-frequency transmission waves always penetrate better than lower frequency waves.

Audio

Another consideration is whether or not you need a soundtrack to be transmitted along with the image. Consider this carefully, because under many circumstances, it is illegal to intercept the oral communications of a person, even though it is legal to record video images of the person. For instance, if you had a security system on your home and had it posted that "these premises record video and audio," you would be relatively safe in collecting any video and audio evidence by tape and preserving it for a possible court case. On the other hand, if you took a wireless audio-equipped video camera and hid it in someone's bedroom or bathroom, where they have an expectation of privacy, both the video and the audio would be illegal, and you could wind up in jail. Unless you absolutely have a legal need to record audio, then simply buy a wireless video camera. There are many circumstances where it is not necessary to post any type of warning that a camera is in use. Your home or property is fine, the bathroom is not. It all hinges on the "expectation of privacy" law, and of course, common sense.

Always observe the particular laws of your state regarding audio and video recording. One of the best sources for wireless video systems and Nanny Cams is a website called Super Circuits, located at www.supercircuits.com. Super Circuits offers some nifty video items, including a smoke detector, a plug-in wall deodorizer, a wall clock, a clock radio, a desk lamp, a necktie, a baseball cap, and many other covert wireless camera systems.

Make Sure the System Fits the Scene

Many of these systems are designed to run off a 9-volt battery and/or a DC/AC plug in. Whichever system you decide to use, remember it should fit with the environment that you intend to use it in. If you're going to be outside walking along the beach, in a bar, or a shopping mall, you may want to consider the spy-cam cell phone. This is a dummy cellular phone case, hollowed out to contain a camera and

9-volt battery. To use it, you need to have a second person carry the recorder and receiver in a bag, or it can be stashed at a nearby location while you walk around with the wireless cell phone in your hand. Little does anyone know that every time you set it down or point it in their direction, it's actually videotaping all of the events.

If you're on a budget, you may want to purchase the wireless camera alone and then install it in your own covert cover. I've even seen these wireless cameras installed in a can of hairspray that sits on a shelf or inside a pack of cigarettes lying on a table.

Technical Considerations

Another thing you have to consider is the field of view on the camera. Most of the pinhole camera lenses come with a 110-degree field of view, some more, some less. A camera with a 110-degree field of view can be positioned in the upper corner of a room, and record almost the entire scene. However, the distance needs to be relatively close, thirty feet or less, in order to use these cameras for any degree of high definition. Remember, these lenses are designed to take in a wide area and not to magnify for distance.

The next consideration when purchasing a wireless cam is the light-gathering ability of the camera. Light-gathering ability is commonly expressed in "lux"—the lower the lux number on the camera, the more low light capable that camera is. An example: a common camera may be rated at 3 lux. If you find a camera that is rated at 1 lux, it will work in much lower light than the 3-lux unit. The best cameras are rated at 0 lux or something on the order of .03 lux. That's getting down into the night-vision spectrum.

The newest chip, which has been developed by Sony, is known as a HAD chip. This HAD chip will film down into levels of darkness that previously required infrared lighting to catch an image. If you are lucky enough to locate one of these newer units with a HAD chip, by all means choose that one, even if it costs a few bucks more.

When purchasing these tiny wireless cams, they are available in both black-and-white and color. There's not much difference in the quality of either, because after all, we're recording images and events for legal purposes, not art. However, you should note that in general, the black-and-white cameras tend to work better in low light, and they usually cost less.

When it comes to batteries for these devices, do not scrimp—buy the very best, highest capacity, 9-volt battery you can buy, such as Duracell or Energizer. You'll be glad you did. If you are going to need to plant a wireless device that is self-powered for any length of time, you may have to use a bigger battery pack. An example would be to take a combination of AA or C cells and use those to power your camera. In other words, six AA or C cells at one point at 5 volts is going to equal the 9 volts you need for your camera, but it is going to have a lot more storage power and therefore a lot longer lasting power than the 9-volt you were using. The problem, of course, becomes size—where can you hide such a large battery pack with this tiny camera? So it becomes a trade-off—the need to be completely hidden verses longer power capacity.

Camera Range

Most video cameras that advertise a 1,500-foot range will be lucky to reach 100 feet in city environments. The range rating on the camera that you purchase is normally measured in a clear, wide-open space, such as a football field. Anytime a single bush gets between you and the receiver it cuts down your signal. A wall, a house, a car, or a tree is going to drastically cut it even more. Also, metal will reflect the signal. In other words, you're not going to have very much success trying to use one of these inside a metal car or truck or, for that matter, some buildings that have a lot of steel and metal supports in the wall. This will drastically cut the signal down.

In my experience, most cameras will dependably go about 100 feet under city conditions and if you get the 800 milliwatts unit (or above), you can probably be assured of at least a block. There are ways to increase the range of these little cameras, and while we cannot increase the transmit power, due to FCC regulations and engineering design, what we can do is increase the size of the receiver antenna.

Super Circuits does sell larger antennas, which will triple the range of your unit. See their antenna section for the types of antennas available, depending on your type of frequency and system. For you bargain hunters out there, don't overlook some of the deals on eBay. You'll be amazed at how many spy cameras are for sale there. I've seen complete systems for sale on eBay as cheap as $29, which includes the camera, the transmitter, and the receiver, and all necessary hookup cables.

Recording the Images

Here's where you will need to spend some money. You may have purchased a $39 wireless spy cam and receiver, but how do you record the images for evidence?

In the past, there were limited choices. You either hook up your receiver into a video machine and record onto a VHS tape, or you had to purchase an 8mm deck. Either choice is not necessarily cheap. While the VHS unit is probably the cheapest, it's very outdated and always requires an AC outlet nearby to power it. Besides that, it's big, bulky, and hard to hide. The 8mm deck, on the other hand, is about the size of a Sony Walkman, but it costs about $500 or more. But the most recent technology is the PVR, or personal video recorder.

PVR Machines

These range in price from about $150 to $500, depending or storage capacity and other features. The main advantage of the PVR is that many are the size of a standard microcassette recorder, and you can easily slide one in your pocket. They also have video and audio "in" jacks where you can hook your receiver up from your wireless video system, and receive the signals from your tiny camera, which is planted somewhere watching your spouse or dishonest employee.

The PVR records in one of two ways: to a hard drive or to an SD chip. The high-end units actually have a 20-gigabyte hard drive and some even as high as 100 gigabytes. The video image is recorded in MPEG-4 format to the hard drive and then downloaded to your computer or laptop, generally with a simple drag-and-drop motion.

The less expensive PVRs use an SD chip. Currently, those chips are available in capacities as high as 512 megabytes. A 512-megabyte chip will hold several hours of video footage. Two SD units that come to mind are the RCA Lyra RD2780 which retails for around $500, and the Mustek PVR-A1, which retails for about $150. Either one of these units has the ability to record video from any source, such as a TV, camcorder, or spy cam. You can look over the Mustek model at www.mustek.com. Many times, you will see the RCA Lyra and the Mustek model available for sale on eBay.

It's my belief that the PVR will be the cutting edge of the future in video as far as spy cams and surveillance go. This is the first time that we have been able to reduce the recorder for a video system down to a manageable size that can actually be carried on a person covertly. As a side note: Most of these PVRs also double as an MP3 player, a still camera, a tape recorder, and some even have video games in them.

One rather novel device I discovered is known as the EZ Witness. The EZ Witness is a personal-security digital-video recorder. It's a small box that has a built-in SD chip to record the video and it has a motion detector built into the unit. You take this stand-alone unit, place it in a room, activate it, and the only time that it comes on is when it detects motion and it begins filming whatever is going on in the room. There's no VCR to set up or any software to install. It records digitally fast-action snapshots automatically when motion is detected. You can play it back on your TV, it's that simple! The EZ Witness is a color camera with a 64-megabyte flash ram for motion or constant recording at a resolution of 640 x 480 or 320 x 240 mode. This unit sells for $225 and is available at www.cctvwholsalers.com. It is about the size of a pack of cigarettes.

THE LIQUOR STORE CAPER

HIS FOREHEAD WAS beaded with dripping sweat as he squirmed in his chair, trying to avoid my gaze. His eyes kept darting to the stack of videotapes in my open briefcase on the table. Carl's caper was about to come apart like a cheap pair of shoes at a Sunday picnic.

Bob and Shirley, the owners of a liquor store, had hired me three weeks prior. They had retired to Florida, gotten bored, and bought a small liquor store on the island for something to do. Bob had owned it now for six months, and the inventory and cash were not balancing. Bob suspected that Carl, a retired cop, had decided to become a "silent partner" and was dipping into the till. Carl had worked for a few years at the store and stayed on when Bob took it over.

I met Bob late one night after closing hours at the store, and he watched as my assistant and I began setting up a hidden wireless-video pinhole camera. I climbed the ladder and removed a ceiling tile, made a pinhole in the material and duct-taped the tiny camera in place on the tile. I reinstalled the tile and went into Bob's private office to set up the recorder and receiver. Bob's office would be locked in his absence, so the recorder would run undetected in his locked office. Each day before Carl came on shift, Bob would insert a fresh tape.

After three weeks of hidden video, we now knew where Bob's cash and inventory were going. I had seven full tapes of Carl working the store and closing up each night. The tiny camera in the ceiling had filmed the checkout counter and most of the room. That's the beauty of using an overhead location and a camera with a 110-degree field of view.

Carl had a pretty crafty game going on, and the tape showed him ringing a No Sale to open the drawer, charging the customer, and putting the cash in the drawer. Then, he would transfer a pack of free matches on the counter from one container to another. At the end of his shift, he counted the matchbooks in container number two, and pocketed a sum of cash equal to his accounting system. One tape showed Carl going out to his car to get his golf bag. He brought it in and during slow times, would practice putting on the carpet in front of the checkout counter. Before he left that night, he filled his golf bag with expensive whiskey and rolled the golf bag out to his car.

To confront him, Bob devised a plan for Carl to come in on Saturday to help move some shelves. What Carl didn't know is that I would be waiting for him in the back room, dressed in a black leather trench coat, to introduce him to the world of private eyes and hidden cameras.

Carl smiled as Bob introduced me and I handed him my card. I asked him to sit down at the table and launched into my talk about shortage problems in retail operations as Carl started telling me about how he was a retired cop and understood where I was coming from.

I was about to drive that understanding to a higher level like a New York taxi driver at rush hour. Carl looked perplexed as I inserted the golf bag videotape into the player and said, "Let me show you an example from a recent case, Carl." That's when he began to sweat.

And, he was literally dripping wet by the time I shut off the tape, and began to fall apart. He did not know that all I had for evidence on the actual cash theft was $90, and of course, the golf-bag booze theft. I looked at Carl as he avoided my gaze and glanced at the door. I told Carl he could go home, that he had twenty-four hours to come back and give Bob a cashier's check for everything he had stolen in the last six months, or he would be charged with theft. I had purposely planted a huge stack of blank, labeled videotapes in my briefcase to make Carl think he had been taped much more than he had. Carl left the store shaken and apologizing.

The next day, Bob called me and was thrilled with the outcome. Carl had come back and given Bob a check for a little over three grand, along with a letter about how he had fallen prey to some overdue bills and turned to drinking and dipping in the till. I was paid $800 for the job, but Bob could have bought the wireless cam for $100 and saved $700 if he had done it himself, since he had his own recording deck.

EIGHT

HOW TO SHAKE A TAIL

SUPPOSE YOU THINK you're being followed. Maybe your wife doesn't trust you, your coworker hates your guts and wants to find evidence that you're working a second secret job, or your father wants to prove that your boyfriend and you are smoking pot. How do you shake the inquiring minds you think may be lurking behind the windshield of that SUV that keeps appearing in your rearview mirror? There are a few sure ways to find out if your suspicions are true and some tricks of the trade for losing that uninvited voyeur. Consider the following statistics:

- **Number of reported stalking cases in United States each year: 1,006,970**

- **Number of women battered yearly: 6,000,000**

- **Percentage of murdered women each year killed by a current or former spouse: 52**

- **Percentage of clients who come to me because they want to avoid being followed: 3**

Let me make very clear that this chapter is *not* intended for a person who is being stalked by strangers or trying to evade known pursuers who pose a physical threat. There are many cases where your first move is to call the authorities. Also, this chapter is not intended for those trying to escape from the law. If, however, there is no physical threat, you're more than likely on your own and need some tactics to avoid being spied upon.

Although the percentage of clients seeking advice about how to evade a tail and/or the services of a private investigator to accomplish this is low (about 2 or 3 percent), the cases are usually high profile. When Paul Reubens (a.k.a. Pee Wee Herman) had to appear in court for lewd behavior in Sarasota, Florida, I was hired to provide his security to and from the courthouse and to lose any tails, and make sure the place he was staying was kept secret. We got into the courthouse without anyone getting a picture—or even a sighting—of him. Getting him out and back to his hotel without detection was more challenging. My adversaries in this case were *Hard Copy*, *Entertainment Tonight*, and all of the major networks. But by using the techniques I share in this chapter, we were able to identify the vehicles tailing us, take evasive maneuvers to lose all the experienced media hacks, and arrive covertly back at Mr. Reubens' hotel room undiscovered.

When we needed to get him into the courthouse undetected by the paparazzi, we hired a big black limo with tinted windows, had the driver arrive at the courthouse at his scheduled appearance time of 9:00 a.m., stop his limo at the main entrance of the courthouse, and approach the rear passenger door. Then, the driver appeared to realize the rush of press, and he pulled the limo a block away, as if to take the inhabitant to a side entrance. While the press was sprinting after the limo, I casually drove the van to the courthouse's basement entrance and myself, Pee Wee, and the bodyguards entered without a single camera nearby.

As in other kinds of cases, I always learn a lot about how to evade detection from my toughest cases. I was once hired to follow a local physician who was in the midst of a divorce. The wife and husband had separated, and he consistently stated there had been no infidelity, but his wife suspected that he was carrying on an affair. Prior to calling me, she had hired several other detective agencies. She requested that we start our surveillance at his office. She did not know where he was residing—only that he disappeared every day at 5:00 p.m. until the next day.

We set up outside the good doctor's office at 5:00 p.m. and waited for the rabbit to leave the hole. Soon thereafter, he jumped into his BMW and headed immediately for the interstate. At this point, both of our tail cars fell in behind him and followed him to an on-ramp, where he pulled into heavy traffic and started heading south. Our usual plan in a case like this is that once we hit the interstate, we shift one of the tail vehicles to ahead of the target. That way we have someone leading and the tail car can drop back to being barely in view of the subject. However, in this case, we were in for quite a surprise. After getting up to a speed of approximately 70 mph, the doctor opened up that BMW and took off. We gave up when our speedometer topped out at 115 mph, and the BMW was going much faster than that.

We went back the second day, this time with three tail cars and a motorcycle. Once again, our target headed southbound on the interstate. At this point, we had prepped the motorcycle for high speeds and were prepared for the possible tickets that might be issued. We already made it clear to our client that she was going to pay the ticket if it resulted in a huge fine. Meanwhile, the doctor had several radar detectors on his dash. It looked like a stealth-fighter control panel.

We hit the interstate, and as we approached 100 miles per hour, I tucked down behind the short windscreen on the motorcycle and prepared for the inevitable. The other cars had dropped back to 80 mph. I followed him approximately forty-two miles, and he never dropped below 115 mph until he reached his exit on the interstate. I could smell success in the wind. I thought I had this asshole.

We entered local city traffic at a normal speed and then the doctor made a right turn, then another, then another, and finally, after the fourth right turn with me on his bumper, I knew I'd been made. At the last stop sign, the doctor waved to me in his rearview mirror as I was stuck behind a vehicle turning left. There was no point in continuing. This guy was just too slick.

We followed the doctor on two other occasions and were never successful in finding his final destination or girlfriend. We suggested that the only way to follow him was by airplane, but the client didn't want to foot the bill.

We later identified his girlfriend through the doctor's office phone records. It was 1987, and the technology for electronic surveillance was just emerging. After tracking the girlfriend's address through phone records and a public-records search, we were able to use a stationary van in the neighborhood and videotape the doctor's arrival, spending the night, and leaving the next morning. The wife used this tape to confront the husband with his affair and interestingly enough, the husband and wife got back together. Ten years later, she was back in my office. They were separating once more, and she wanted us to track his activity again.

CONFIRM AND/OR EVADE A TAIL ON THE ROAD

THE SAME FREAKIN' Toyota Camry with the bobblehead dog on the dashboard has just moved from the left and pulled behind you two car lengths back. Could that be the same one you noticed yesterday pulling out of a side street behind you? You've been on the alert since you found your cell phone moved while you were showering. Your better half may be suspicious. Or you know the company thinks you're not making all of the client stops you should. Or, do you fear your father is having you followed even though you're a grown child legally free to squander your trust fund any way you want?

Although it's not true of all of them, many of the techniques below can be used to both confirm that you're being tailed and, at the same time, discourage the tail. Once you've made the tail and he or she knows it, they usually have to quit for the day. If it's a private eye, he or she is going to return with a different vehicle and a different approach. If it was an amateur with fewer resources, you may have lost your tail for good.

Make a U-turn

Head for the nearest four-lane highway. After a short distance, maneuver to the left lane and look for the first available break in the median strip where you can safely do a u-turn. Immediately after you perform your u-turn, watch the rearview mirror constantly until the point where you made the u-turn is totally out of sight. Naturally, you're looking for any vehicle that makes the same u-turn behind you.

When a predator or investigator is faced with this choice or dilemma, he or she has to choose to stay with you and risk exposure or pull off for the day and change vehicles. Either you've made the tail and/or discouraged them for today.

Head for a Dead End

If you suspect that the car behind you is a tail and you would like to confirm this, one of the best methods is to head for the nearest dead-end street. By all means, don't do this if you think there is any element of danger involved. Enter the dead-end, go to the last residence and pull into the driveway. Your tail will follow you in an effort to identify who you're visiting. Once you see the car enter the dead-end street, you now have the pursuer in a bottleneck. Put your car in reverse and head back out the street. At this point, you're in a position where you can either confront the person or you can fall in behind him or her and take their tag number. The predator has to pass you within a few feet.

Your tail knows the jig is up, and with the tag number you can identify who the driver is. If the tag comes back a licensed PI, go to the heading on page 233 entitled Call Your Lawyer and take the steps described therein.

Residential Turns

A good method for detecting a tail in a residential area involves paying attention. If you make three consecutives turns in a residential area and the same car is still behind you, the chances are you're under surveillance. Make a u-turn to shake the tail.

Left Turns

Head down most congested roadways and make left turns as many times as necessary to shake the tail. Allow just enough time to get across two lanes of traffic before the next hoard of cars. This move is more successful where there is no stop sign or stop light. You want to leave the tail stalled and unable to follow you because he or she can't get across the extra lanes due to heavy traffic flow.

For Sale Sign

If you're in a residential area, keep a sharp eye out for the first house with a For Sale sign. As long as the tail is not within view, back your car into the driveway (or better yet, the carport) shut off the ignition, and lay down on the front seat. Wait until the pursuer goes by or wait ten or twenty minutes and head in the opposite direction. This may give you a chance to write down identifying details about the pursuit car and driver, especially tags. Most investigators will pull off once they've lost you for more than ten minutes.

The Yellow Light

Another method, if you can gauge your speed, is to go through on yellow traffic lights, leaving the pursuer with the choice of running a red light, having an accident, or coming to a stop. If you can get a tail stopped at a red light, then you immediately want to turn off the roadway, get lost back in residential streets, and stay there for at least thirty minutes.

Look for a Second Tail

Because you've identified a possible tail behind you and have successfully used one of these maneuvers to lose that cowboy, do not overlook the fact that there may be two or three tails on you at this point. Even if you shake one, begin looking for other vehicles that are consistently in your proximity.

Collect Evidence of a Tail

If you think you've seen the same car pull out and follow you again today or the same van parked across from where you work for the third time this week, go on the offensive. To confirm you're not making this up, write down any details about the car—make, year, and model of the car; license number; body damage; prominent antennae; the appearance of the driver. Also note the time and date. If you have written down the direction of travel and time of day when you began to suspect you're being followed, these notes may become important later in a court of law.

CONFIRM AND/OR EVADE A PEDESTRIAN TAIL

The Circle

One of the best ways to confirm a tail on foot is to walk in a circle. There is no legitimate reason for someone to follow you in a circle. Most people are interested in going from point A to B. Look the person in the eye. Even if they fail to meet your gaze, if they were following you, they'll assume they've been made and retreat.

Find Open Space

Wander to an open area and watch for anyone who appears to be loitering.

Approach the Mark

Here you're looking for an evasive measure on the part of the person you think might be following you. This is a giveaway. In a well-populated area, pretend you're going to approach the tail. Most skilled investigators don't want you close enough for recognition because you'll remember them, and they'll perform an evasive measure. If it looks like someone is approaching me, I immediately turn and talk to someone. For example, I stop a pedestrian and ask directions—anything to discourage the contact.

If a person reacts this way, it could mean that that person is following you. Especially if the suspicious person asks for directions more than once. That's a giveaway. Turn and leave.

NOTIFY THE AUTHORITIES WHEN APPROPRIATE

Call Local Law Enforcement

This is not rocket science. If you are in physical danger either from someone you know or a stranger, you need to put down this book and notify the police. Don't try to handle a potentially life-threatening situation by yourself. It could be an angry spouse, neighbor, lover, or co-worker who is lurking in your rearview mirror, following you down the aisles of the grocery store or peeking through your windows. If this person has harmed you in the past, threatened you, or poses a threat, it's time to alert the cops and your lawyer, and take precautions.

Ditto if you realize someone you don't know is shadowing you. Of course, the stranger could be a private eye. If you're in a contested divorce, any kind of personal dispute, or embroiled in a civil case, the stranger you've noticed could be a private investigator. However, if you've run the tags, and this person is not a licensed PI, you need to report your stalker to local law enforcement and alert family members, as this could be a danger to yourself or your family.

Call Your Lawyer

If the stranger following you turns out to be a private eye, there's a typical scenario you can employ using your attorney to make the dick back off.

I'm assuming that you have identified the private eye. You then need to proceed to your lawyer's office and have him or her contact the licensing bureau of the state in which you reside. He or she will obtain the agency address for the PI and the investigator's license number. Your attorney will then write a letter to the PI, threatening a lawsuit for harassment of his or her client. The lawyer will normally go on to say that the activity this investigator is involved in has become obvious to their client and that no court of law could interpret his actions as those of a "reasonable investigation." The continued shadowing and harassing of the client has turned into "no more than a threatening pursuit causing great mental anguish to the client." I'm quoting from actual letters I've received, and upon receipt of a letter of this nature, we immediately terminate following the target. A target can actually file a harassment suit against a PI.

Hire a Private Investigator

If you're unable to get the attention you want from law enforcement and/or you can't get the tag number or identity of the investigator you think has been following you, it may be time to call your own private eye to tail the tail. This may cost between $500 and $2,000 to make a tail.

ADOPT EVASIVE MEASURES

YOU KNOW YOU'RE being followed, but have no real legal recourse to stop it. So take charge, and take measures to evade the asshole who's making your life miserable. You are at an advantage because you know someone is following you. Private investigators dread that moment when their work becomes so much harder. And it's good to be prepared for evasive measures by car and by foot, since, if you're like most humans, you'll be traveling in both modes.

But that's where you're going to stop acting like most humans. Most people are creatures of habit and chances are, if you leave your house at the same time every day, you will take the same route for at least a short distance. As an investigator, we rely on these patterns, as most tails are never solved on the first attempt. The most difficult targets to shadow are the ones who are on alert and taking the following precautions.

Evasive Measures Traveling by Car

In addition to the evasive measures recommended while driving on the road, you might have success with any one of the following evasive tactics. You're limited only by your imagination.

One of the techniques I used in the Pee Wee Herman case is probably not for the do-it-yourselfer unless you have some brave friends. Although we successfully got Herman to the courthouse every day, the most difficult part was getting him home from the courthouse so no one knew where he was staying. We used two separate cars that followed Pee Wee as he left the courthouse for his private condo out on the beach.

During the route of travel, we had the two tails act as blockers. At an intersection as the car with Pee Wee passed on through, the two blockers blocked the route of travel by pulling up side-by-side at the intersection. One driver faked car trouble and raised his hood while the other pulled next to him, apparently trying to jump-start his car. Be prepared for the horns from the infuriated cars behind you. The reporters and photographers sat there in frustration.

Another time, when we left the courthouse and headed over the bridge to the barrier island where Pee Wee was staying, I had both blocker cars turn their cars sideways and block the entire bridge at the center span. The police couldn't possibly get to the center of the bridge, so my blockers were safe for approximately ten minutes while I whisked him out of sight.

Vary Your Routine

Start varying your times of travel and routes for leaving the house. In other words, become unpredictable. This becomes very confusing to investigators.

Vary the Vehicle

If you have access to multiple vehicles, use different cars, but make sure you're not creating a pattern.

The Switch

This method is a bit elaborate and involves another person. One of the best ways to prevent a tail is to stop it before it begins. A favorite way to do this is have a friend of the same stature and build visit you at your location wearing contrasting clothing. If you're in a business suit, have that person enter the house wearing jeans and a T-shirt. Before doing this, make sure you've walked outside and checked the mail or retrieved the paper in your business suit to give the tail a good look at what you're wearing.

When your friend arrives, switch out clothing. Have your friend drive away in your vehicle, and as you see the tail pursuing your car, wait about ten minutes, exit and drive away in your friend's car for your covert meeting.

The Crowd Ruse

Another method is to invite several people over, with several people in each vehicle. This makes it difficult, as everyone is leaving, to determine which car you entered and which group you're with. Often, in the confusion, the investigator will follow the wrong car. This happens a lot at night when following a teenager from a party. It's hard to tell which car he or she got into.

The Second Car

A simple evasive maneuver when you're being watched while you're at home or at another location involves borrowing a second car. Park your car in front of a workplace or friend's house. Leave undetected in the borrowed car of a coworker or friend. The odds are that the investigator will be watching your vehicle at a hair salon or at your office, waiting for you to return to it.

Blow the Whistle

If you suspect a car is watching you from a fixed location, have a friend report a suspicious vehicle on the street. While the investigator is being grilled by police, you're driving away in your own vehicle with a smile on your face to meet your lover or contact.

Evasive Tactics on Foot

You know you're being followed as you walk down the main street of town. You've made the clown. To evade surveillance, your location, of course, dictates your choices. In a busy city, you can escape by hailing a passing taxi. But not everyone is facile enough to get lost in the subway system or jump on public transportation just ahead of the pursuer. That's in the movies. If the opportunity occurs, great, but don't include those sorts of maneuvers in your plan of action. Here are some things you can do in a small town or a big city.

Carry a Simple Disguise

Carry a bag with extra clothing. It doesn't have to be too elaborate—a cap, a jacket that contrasts, different sunglasses. Someone may go as far as wearing shorts and a T-shirt under slacks and long sleeves. You can step into a restroom and totally change appearance. You can also wear old things so you can discard them in the rest room. Now walk out without a bag. Change your hair and put on a cap and different sunglasses.

The Flash Camera

If you think you may be followed on foot at night, carry a cheap flash camera with you. When you turn around, point the camera at the person and hit the flash button. This will cause the pursuer to lose his night vision. It will take up to five minutes for their eyes to adjust. Not only can you can escape, but you now have a photo as well.

Entering a Multistory Building

You can enter a multistory building, then enter the elevator. The pursuer should wait outside the elevator and record what floor you're stopping at. If they don't get in the elevator with you, push every floor on the elevator. If they do get in with you, stop at a floor, start to get out, then change your mind as if you made a mistake. See if your pursuer reacts the same way.

Shake a Tail in a Store

Go in a store entrance and out the back. If your pursuer follows you in the store, walk up to the clerk and say you thought you saw the person shoplift. Head for an exit and he'll try to leave too. Your goal is that he's stopped. In most cases, security will detain him while you get away.

We were once hired to tail a woman whose evasive maneuver (it's a good one) was based on going shopping. She had been caught by PIs before, so she was a wary cookie. The first morning, we set up on her home and two tail cars fell in behind her as she left her neighborhood and parked at the local shopping mall. So far, this represented no suspicious activity; she was doing what she told her husband she would do. We assumed this was another easy surveillance. One agent followed her on foot in case she was seeing someone who worked in the shopping center.

After watching her browse through the lingerie section in Saks and thinking all was going as planned, the agent watched as the target suddenly walked to the rear exit of the store and stepped out the door. Our agent stood there with her jaw dropped as we watched our client's wife step into a waiting taxicab and fade out of sight. There was no time to contact the agent on the other side of the mall to engage the target. This did not make our client happy.

We eventually caught this woman, but we had to get very clever. Our client had deliberately gone out of town for the weekend to give her the golden opportunity to carry on her affair. We followed her as she drove her Mercedes to a grocery store and shut off her lights. It only took twenty seconds for the door of the white sports car parked next to her to open; a boy toy half her age jumped out, entered her rear passenger door, and laid down on the seat. If we hadn't been watching as closely as we did, we would have never caught her.

She backed out immediately and we followed her back to her residence. At home, she used the remote garage-door opener, pulled into the garage, and lowered the door. They spent the night in her home with no one the wiser except us.

NINE

MISSING PERSONS

DAVE WAS A homeless man about forty-five years old. His parents contacted me from Vero Beach, Florida, because they hadn't heard from their son during Christmas. A Vietnam vet, Dave had basically dropped out of the system and off the radar screen years ago. The parents had an address in Bradenton, in a trailer park where Dave said he lived. But they had never been there, because he only agreed to meet them at a restaurant during Christmas. The rest of the time, Dave's life was reclusive and unknown to them. The parents were worried that something had happened to him, as this was the first Christmas he had not contacted them. They supplied me with a couple of old photographs of Dave and the trailer park where he was supposed to be.

I went to the trailer park and spoke to the manager, who had neither heard of Dave nor recognized the photograph. A check of all the fancy databases only showed that Dave used a general-delivery address at the local post office. I went to the zip code area of the post office and began to cruise the alleys and backstreets. At specific corners, I put up wanted posters offering a $50 reward for anyone who saw "Homeless Dave" and a toll-free number for them to call. The toll-free number is important when you're dealing with investigation work. The toll-free number can be gotten from your own phone company for as little as $5 a month. This will give you an 800 number that rings in to any phone that you would like to have it assigned to. It was through this number that I was able to locate him.

After a few days, I received a call from a man at a pay phone who claimed that he knew Dave and had seen the reward poster. I went and met with the man, "Carlos," who was obviously a street person and had no address himself. Before I shelled out $50 to this character, I was going to make sure that the information he was giving me was good. I put him in the car and he drove with me to a local department store on a main roadway. Behind the department store was a small stretch of bushes and woods. Carlos pointed down a footpath and told me that Homeless Dave had a tent set up back in the palmettos, where he had been living for the last two years. I locked my car and had Carlos stand outside while I trekked up through the foot path. The path was littered with wine bottles, beer cans, and all the debris you might expect to find in a hobo jungle. Rounding a corner, I came up on a small pup tent and approached the camp. The camp was vacant at the time, but I could see that someone had been living there on a regular basis. I gave Carlos (my snitch) half of the $50 bill, told him to call me in two days, and that once I had confirmed it was Dave, I would give him the other half. That evening, at about 6:00, I was setting up surveillance on the tent when I observed Homeless Dave heading up the footpath to the tent. I didn't approach Dave, because I didn't want him to strike camp and run. I had no idea what he was hiding from. I did contact Dave's parents and let them know that I had located Dave and what the situation was. They thanked me and that closed the case. I cashed the $500 check and moved on to the next file.

Approximately two days later, Carlos called me and I arranged to meet him to give him the other half of his fifty. No sooner had I returned to my office and my phone rang again from another pay phone booth. I picked it up and it was Homeless Dave, and he was pissed as hell. Apparently, Dave had seen his wanted poster on a street sign and was angry that someone was looking for him. I explained the situation, that it was his mother and his father, and requested that he call them. Dave became a little less aggravated once he learned that it was Mom and Dad looking for him and he promised that he would call them. I did hear from the parents the following day, who reported that Dave had called and they were on their way to meet him.

Homeless cases are some of the toughest cases to work because there's generally no paper trails of the person you're looking for. You have to resort to creative and novel ideas such as wanted posters at strategic zones, checking with the Salvation Army, and checking with local missions, in order to start finding a thread or clues that lead you to your target.

But it may not be a missing family member you're seeking. While locating a missing person can be as serious as finding a kidnapped child, a runaway, and a birth mother, it can also be as frivolous as locating that old sweetheart from ten years earlier. Ten percent of my business is locating missing persons. Runaway teenagers also comprise a percentage of my business. The way the laws are set up today, when you report your teenager missing, the authorities don't actively start to search for your child. Their excuse is that "most are runaways." They never begin in sooner than twenty-four hours unless the child is younger than thirteen. If the missing child is a teenager, they won't look for a couple of days. It's police policy, not law. That can be very frustrating. So it's good to know how and where to start.

In this chapter, I'll show you how to conduct your own investigation for a missing teen by properly searching your child's room for clues and tracing recent telephone use. For example, even if you don't have caller ID, you can use a tape recorder to record the tones from the teenager's last call. Using a tone decoder, you can then turn sounds into a physical number. This is the only way to recover the last call made by the missing person. I'll outline how to use photographs, handouts, posters, rewards, and license plate numbers. I'll show you how to canvas neighborhoods and convenience stores where the missing teen might be. Even if they're hiding in the woods, teens usually go to the local 7-11 for a soft drink.

As I said, not all missing persons are children. You might want to find a tenant, anyone that owes you money, a runaway spouse, or the key witness who saw the accident two years ago. You'll employ different tactics, like those outlined in Chapter 3 using public records. For example, to find a runaway tenant, the first thing you'll do is hit that trash can before the garbage man. They often throw away road maps or notes about their new destination. We'll also give you the script of a pretext for interviewing a relative who may be conned into revealing the new address for the missing person.

I will describe some of my actual cases and outline techniques you can use to request records going back decades. I located a birth mother with only a name and birth date by contacting the department of motor vehicles in the most likely states of residence. In most states, if you write to the department of motor vehicles with a name and birth date, you can confirm a current address and driver's license number. This is public record. Our client now had the option of a reunion with her biological mother.

A high percentage of my business, however, involves children kidnapped in a custody battle. I will show you how to get the best use out of the authorities and their resources, as well as how to locate your missing child using the tricks of the trade. Whatever the nature of your missing person, many of the steps are the same.

Whether it's a family member or an old lover, the chances are you will need to locate someone at least once in your lifetime, and this chapter will save you a lot of money by giving you the basic skills to be able to do it on your own. Missing persons can actually be broken down into three general categories:

- Misplaced Persons. This will be the largest segment of missing persons. This covers things like the missing witness who saw your car accident, the old girlfriend from five years ago who you'd like to see, or perhaps even the brother you haven't heard from for a few years. These are people that are neither missing nor intentionally hiding. They're just misplaced. In others words, they're out there someplace, but you just don't know where they're at.

- Skips. A skip is someone who is hiding from you deliberately. This could be an ex-husband, a fugitive from justice or the guy that owes you twenty grand. He's out there, he's living, he's spending money, enjoying life, and hiding from you and his responsibilities.

- Runaways. Runaways generally are children between the ages of twelve and seventeen. A typical scenario would be for little "Suzy," who went out with "Billy" Friday night, and then failed to come home. You find yourself in a panic Saturday morning, wondering if she's in a ditch somewhere, without a clue on how to begin trying to locate her.

This chapter will guide you through everything from basic steps to some of the more advanced techniques that private investigators use, at a charge of thousands of dollars. Put your wallet away, keep your money for more exciting ventures, and we'll go through them one category at a time.

STEPS FOR FINDING A MISSING PERSON

ANYTIME YOU'RE SEARCHING for a missing person, the very first step is to build an intelligence file as outlined in Chapter 3. Pull together the basics, such as name, date of birth, middle initial, and of course the ever-elusive social security number. We develop our information from people trails as well as paper trails, and with the advent of the Internet, computer trails.

Names

Many times, you will start your search with a vague name, maybe something as simple as Butch, Fred, Susie, or some other nickname coupled with a last name. The first thing you will need to do is to identify which name would normally be found on their driver's license or any other formal identification. If this person is a family member, perhaps interviewing your mother may provide additional clues as to the proper first name and middle initial.

Interviews

When interviewing people of interest, it is important that you do a thorough interview. This is where most investigators fail. Subtle details, such as age range applied to the missing person, can make the difference between success and failure. For example, when interviewing someone, ask them to give you a minimum age and a maximum age for the subject. Ask for a list of any known relatives of the person. Be sure and ask for any nicknames the person is known by and any previous addresses they used in the past, with the time frames if possible. This will become important later for your researching the old city directories and telephone directories.

Male relatives of the subject are particularly important. The reason for this, of course, is that female relatives often get married and change their last name. If the missing person has been missing for a long time, their sister may have been married several times and have several different names, whereas a brother will still be carrying the same name he was born with. Find out if the person has a common occupation that they normally practice. This will assist you in looking at various professional organizations, associations, and memberships. But if the subject you're looking for is male, it is important to ask for the father's name. Often you will find that sons are named after their father, either with the first name or the middle name. Many times you'll find that a female is named after her mother with a first name or middle name. All of these are subtle clues to assist you in finding the person's true identity. Remember, when you research public records, you will be looking at the formal name.

Some areas you should check when looking for a missing person are: last church attended, school attended, last known employer, known friends, next door neighbors, and last known residence, and the local mailman, just to name a few. If you've conducted your interview properly you should be using the subject's full name including middle initial, approximate age, last known residence, spouse's name, date of birth, social security number, list of known relatives, place of last employment, children's names, and perhaps even the name of the family dog. (Hey, who knows, you may want to check animal control for dog-bite records or for a rabies tag.) These forms will also contain information on the dog's owner and perhaps the name of the vet the family used.

Follow the Paper Trail

The first basic thing you can do is to check the local telephone directories for each city in your area. Check for telephone listings under the husband's name or the wife's name. If the person has been known to live in the area for a long time, you might also try calling other persons with the same last name, under the theory that perhaps some of these people are related. If you fail to find your subject using this method, be sure to follow up with a call to directory assistance and ask the operator for a new listing for John Doe. If this fails, the next step will be to mail the subject a letter at the last known address. Send this letter certified with forwarding address requested.

Another trick I have used for getting additional information is to go to the local police department and request any police calls to the last known residence of the subject based on the address, for the last two years. With this tactic, you'll often discover the names of people that were at the home, who are associated with your subject. Many of these police reports will also contain missing elements, such as a date of birth, and on occasion, even the social security number. They'll often also list who filed the complaint. While you're there, go ahead and check parking tickets, traffic tickets, and crash reports.

You can also use the tactics outlined in Chapter 3. Go online and do a public-records search. Go to the clerk of the court, and follow the paper trail of deeds, property sales and purchases, lawsuits, marriages, divorces, and tax information. Check the department of motor vehicles and check for tickets. If you find a recent ticket in Miami for speeding and your subject has been gone for a year from your city, chances are he or she has taken residence up near that location.

Next, head over to the water department and talk to customer service or billing. Many times they will have a new hookup in the subject's name, or a forwarding address for the old bill. When talking to the billing department, pretend you are trying to collect an old bill—they can relate to that and will find some common ground in your situation.

Casing the Hood

Take a trip to the subject's old residence. While there, dig through the garbage can for clues, such as notes, maps, phone numbers, and the names of known creditors who may also be searching for them. The best time of day to do this visit will be about 6:00 p.m. That is when most neighbors will be home and you can go interview them. Be sure and ask if they saw a moving or rental truck at the residence and if so, the name of the company and the color of the truck. A call to the truck and trailer rental places may turn up a truck rental and the destination it is bound for. When talking to the neighbors, you may want to add that you are trying to find them to get a check to the subject from some insurance company or settlement matter. Be sure and get phone numbers from people as you go along. This will allow you to call back with other questions and to check for further information.

Web Searching

As mentioned in Chapter 3, the Internet can be a major time-saver when searching for missing persons. Go to www.google.com and click on the Advanced tab. Try entering the name of the person in the Exact section and enter such things as city name, occupation, hobby, state, and various topics related to the subject you are looking for. If that fails, use combinations such as "Pat Smith" instead of "Patrick Smith" on the Exact section. This search will turn up everything, from news articles about your subject to trade publications and court cases. See Chapter 3 for more details.

In the summer of 2003, I had a client, "William," who retained me to locate two missing persons. Now eighty-two years old, William had served in World War II. In 1943, his military travels landed him for a brief time at the Port of Tampa, Florida. While there, a young couple with two children befriended him and treated him kindly. He never forgot their kindness, and now, sixty years later, he wanted to try to locate them. He was nearly certain that the parents, who were a bit older than him, were probably deceased. But the children had been twelve and thirteen at the time, so he thought we might be able to locate them.

William supplied me with the first and last names of the parents, and the first names of the children. I searched the social security death database and found that both the mother and the father were deceased. This search was free over the Internet and can be accessed by anyone with a computer. I knew that in seeking the children involved in this case that the easiest person to find would be the boy, because he would most likely have retained the family surname. Fortunately, his first and last name were unusual, which made the search easier than if I would have had a name like John Smith. Using the Internet, I logged onto www.locateplus.com, and ran a search based on first and last name only, which generated approximately 100 names. While searching through this list, which cost me exactly a buck, I located a person in Indiana with a matching first and last name, in an age range—the late

60s—of the person I was looking for. Not only was his address present, but his phone number was listed as well. I called "Pete," and he answered the phone. I introduced myself and quizzed him about his mother and father, asking if they had once lived in Tampa. Peter not only confirmed this, but he also remembered the young soldier who had come to visit, and said he would like to meet the soldier again. I contacted my client, who was not only thrilled by the news, but submitted an article to the local newspaper regarding my work and how amazed he was that after sixty-one years, we could go back and find someone with as little to work with as a first and last name. It is certainly the longest time period I've had to work with on a missing persons case.

Wildcard Searching

If all you have is rough information on your subject, you may want to have a "wildcard" search by a local PI. You give him or her the name, age range, zodiac sign, any combinations you have, and ask the PI to run a list of persons for you with their address. You can then take this list and make your own calls to narrow it down and do the legwork the PI would normally charge for by the hour. One place to request special searches of this nature is www.abika.com.

You can target a given area, such as a city or state, or even nationwide, as a geographic area. For example, you can ask the system to give you a list of all persons in the United States with a first name of Robert and a middle initial of M who are between forty-five and forty-eight years of age, and were born under Scorpio. A major supplier of this kind of search is Choicepoint, Inc. However, they do not deal with the general public. Many PIs have access to this system when a legitimate legal reason for the data is established. You might also ask a PI to do a nationwide driver's license search based on the name, or a nationwide vehicle search based on a name. Most people in today's world drive or have owned a vehicle.

THE RUNAWAY TEEN

TEENS CAN BE frustrating to find and the best advice is to build your tools in advance of this common event. Otherwise, you will lose a lot of sleep. Here are a few suggestions to help you.

Install caller ID on all your phones and every month write the incoming numbers on your teen's calls down in a notebook. If you do not already have a phone that has a list of dialed numbers on a redial menu, get one. Teens often tell or plan this with a friend of the same age. It will be important to know whom your teen called, or who called them, just before he or she slipped out the window and rode off on the Harley.

If you get your teen a cell phone, try to get one that is GPS enabled. Many providers offer this service today. Nextel is one of them. This system allows you to go online and run a locate, and even shows a map right down to the block they are located in. Another interesting web site is www.wherify.com. This site provides GPS phones and more with what are called "bread crumbing" features. Bread crumbing is a feature that allows you to have the system do a locate at time intervals you set, day or night. This creates a trail to every location they have been, how long they stayed, and when they left. Of course, if you tell them the phone is a GPS tracker, they will ditch the phone and the gig will be up. Use your own judgment on this.

When your teen spends the night with friends or introduces friends, get the father's or mother's name and phone number and make a courtesy call to them. This may help in the future when you ring them at 3:00 a.m., screaming and sobbing about your wayward teen.

Once a month, be sure and do an inspection of your teen's room, address book, notes lying around, and, of course, the teen's computer and web trails. Always know the password to your teen's account on the Internet. Communicate with your teen about where they went and what they did and with whom when they go out. This gives you hang-

THE PRIVATE INVESTIGATOR'S HANDBOOK

outs where people know them and where they may be seen if they run away. It also gives you locations to post pictures and flyers among people who can recognize them on sight.

Finding a Runaway

If anyone knows where your teen is, it is one of his or her friends. The problem is getting the friend to give up your teen and tell you what he or she knows.

If possible, use another teen, possibly one of your other children, to help talk to your missing teen's friends. You are, after all, an adult, and no doubt your teen has created a less than favorable impression of you. Start with the parents of your teen's friend, and make sure you have their blessings in interviewing their child. Most parents will do what they can to help, as they can usually relate to your situation.

Be sure to tell everyone that if they hear from your child, to note the number he or she called from, and if it is an e-mail, to save the e-mail, print out an exact copy, and send it to you. Most e-mails can be traced right down to the server and, many times right to the computer that sent it. Every e-mail has a header that contains an IP (internet provider number). When traced, you'll be able to determine who runs the system and access some information. If you are computer literate, you can trace this IP number yourself by going to www.crimetime.com/online.htm and clicking on the Internet Search tab and then on the ARIN link.

In a recent case, I obtained an e-mail that a runaway sent to his friend and used this site to track him down. The runaway had taken a bus to Orlando and the trail grew cold at that point. The IP number from the e-mail he sent his friend a few days later enabled me to locate the runaway in Los Angeles, of all places. Pretty amazing what a sixteen-year-old can accomplish these days and how far they can travel.

Missing persons is such a huge category that it could fill volumes based on type, circumstances, profile of the person, and more. You can never have too much information when conducting an investigation. The most productive thing you can do is work hard, collecting all you can. Ask a million questions from everyone you consider an interested person. Take photographs of your teen every three months or less, know their SSN, weight, height, favorite haunts, and hobbies. If you have children, chances are it is going to happen, so prepare now and keep the sleepless nights to a minimum when it does. One last note on this: Be constantly looking for security cams at locations your teen is suspected of having been. Many businesses today run time-lapse video, and the manager or security chief may allow you to review the tape. It could show your teen entering a car and even the tag number.

PARENTAL KIDNAPPING

AS I MENTIONED earlier, I am retained quite often to locate children who have been abducted by one of their parents involved in a custody dispute. This is a gray area, one in which I hesitate to go into too much detail, because there are many legal and emotional circumstances and ramifications. Such a case is best left to professionals. However, I will relate how I handled one case. You can use the information at your discretion.

One day, my phone rang. A very deep voice said, "Mr. Chambers, I need your help." The voice belonged to a man by the name of James Alexander, a Philadelphia lawyer. James began to tell me his story and I understood why he was so upset. James had divorced his wife approximately two years prior, and during the course of the divorce, had gotten primary custody of his children from his soon-to-be ex-wife. Things had gone along fairly well for the past two years, when, three months ago, she decided to take the children during a visitation period and disappear. James went on to explain that he had hired several detective agencies in the Philly area but none of them had been able to find her or his kids. James went on to explain that his ex-wife's mother had been running interference and assisting her, and he had also learned that his ex-wife had hooked up with a group of mothers that forms a chain of safe houses for women involved in custodial disputes who run away with their children. These groups assist in hiding them out and, in many cases, even changing their identities for them. Of course, all of this is in direct violation of the court order issued many times in divorce cases. These are ex-spouses who decide that they are going to take their children despite a judge's order.

I started the case by going on the Internet and doing all the typical searches, which only turned up an address history that ended several months previous. Obviously, I had to look for the adult in this case, since there are no paper trails for children that are readily available as public records. I purchased a prepaid phone card from a firm on the Internet. This prepaid phone card was sent to the mother of the parental kidnapper with a nice little introduction letter. Basically, the letter said, "Here's your free $50 phone card for long-distance phone calling to introduce you to ABC phone cards. We hope that you enjoy our services and will continue to purchase the phone card at the following toll-free number." The theory and the strategy here was that the mom would give this toll-free card to her daughter who was on the run, and that when her daughter used this card, we could look at the list of numbers called and get the location of her and the children. Within two weeks, the mother had given the phone card to her daughter for her secret phone calls. We received a list of calls that the card was used for and tracked the kidnapper and the two children to a rural home in the Connecticut countryside. My client, the attorney, notified the police, and within hours, his two children were back in his possession.

It really wasn't that difficult to unravel the case, it was just a matter of employing the right strategy and tactics, and being a little creative. I don't think the FBI appreciated the competition, and hearing that the case was solved by an outsider. I doubt I will be on their dinner-invitation list anytime soon.

APPENDICES

APPENDICES

SECURE THE LEGAL CHAIN OF EVIDENCE

EVIDENCE, WHICH HAS been legally obtained and preserved for your attorney to use in court, is critical to every investigation. Every case hinges on the best proof you can gather. This holds true even if you don't go to court. Often, evidence—for example, panties in a baggie—will be all the leverage you need to settle a civil case in your favor.

Actually, you're really working for your lawyer when you conduct your PI work. And that means securing evidence that he or she can wave about in court. You want solid evidence aimed at the pocketbook or arrogance of your opponent. Our discussion of the collection and preservation of evidence is going to be limited to only documents and exhibits that can be secured and admitted as legal evidence by an amateur or private citizen. This is a huge topic that anyone who watched the O.J. trial will remember is always of concern to law enforcement. However, the information here is basically manageable, and could be critical if you're conducting your own PI work.

Entering the evidence into court is always a challenge because the adverse lawyer will attack the legality and chain of evidence. In this case, the problem is doubly difficult because the evidence collector—you—has an interest in the outcome of the case. A lawyer will try to cast doubt on your credibility and objectivity with the evidence, because you obviously stand to benefit from its admission in the court of law. Therefore, it is very important that you are meticulous in identifying, labeling, dating, initialing, and storing the evidence. Follow the standard methods outlined here carefully, including correctly documenting the source of evidence, maintaining the chain of evidence (remember O. J.'s glove), and correctly storing evidence in a locked secured area (refrigerated where appropriate) to which only you or your attorney has a key. Otherwise, your evidence will be challenged.

You have collected incriminating receipts, e-mail correspondence, bank statements, videotapes, and taped witness statements. You have the goods. In this appendix, I'll share my secrets for documenting, preserving, and storing evidence that will hold up in court. Every piece of evidence needs to be packaged, dated, and stored in a way that won't be open to challenge.

ASSEMBLE AN EVIDENCE-COLLECTION KIT

You will want to have the following handy for a very basic evidence-collection kit to check out a scene, vehicle, or briefcase for physical evidence, and for collecting and retrieving evidence from a scene. Today, evidence can be very microscopic. Many times, it is the little things that count, from a hair follicle to a clothing thread. Gather the following for your kit:

- **Tape measure**

- **Notebook and pens**

- **Plain envelopes of various sizes**

- **Ziploc® bags**

- Labels

- Six-inch ruler

- Permanent marker pen

- Bottle of distilled water

- Camera. Have a still camera with a flash with you at all times to take photos of evidence before you disturb or remove it. Use the flash even for daylight shots. This is known as "fill flash" and eliminates shadows. Be cautious using it on reflective surfaces or it will blur certain pictures such as a fingerprint on glass.

- Flashlight

- Tape recorder. Create a verbal log as you observe and collect evidence from any setting. Make verbal notes describing the condition, weather, location, who is present, time of day, unusual observations, or even questions for later exploration of theory.

- Tweezers or tongs. These are used to pick up articles when it is appropriate to minimize handling. Some items are so small you will need tweezers to collect them, such as threads or hair follicles.

- Cotton swabs. These are to collect stains and liquid, blood, semen, and DNA.

- Latex gloves. Use these to prevent your own prints or DNA from being transferred to evidence.

The list is basic and limited because we are not going to get into any major criminal-evidence collection. That is better left to the police and the experts. Should you locate evidence relevant in a criminal matter, maintain guard over it, secure the area, and call the police or detective in charge of the criminal case. They will have the million-dollar devices and supplies to collect and preserve it properly. This kit and the steps suggested here are for the private citizen conducting private investigations in civil issues, not criminal.

Gathering Evidence at a Scene

Get your flashlight out of the kit. One technique they teach you in the police academy is to shine it at an angle to find things you'd miss. By shining the light across the floor or surface at an angle, it will cause small items to cast a much larger shadow, enabling you to see things you may have otherwise overlooked. Don't use direct lighting. With this method you can find hair follicles, pills (medication or drugs), earrings, rings, other jewelry, credit cards, scraps of paper, and other small personal items someone might have left.

Document the Discovery of Evidence

This is generally done today with a camera, by taking photos of the evidence as you find it and before it has been disturbed. Use a small tape recorder to keep track of your photographic record. Negatives are numbered, so, as you take a picture, speak into the recorder, giving date, time, and view so it will match up to the negatives. For example, "Number one: This is the east view of Susan Brown's house from approximately 100 feet away." You will also need to record that this is a southwest view or whatever direction you are shooting. Also document in your verbal record the circumstances under which evidence was collected. When you get those photos back, the negatives will be in consistent sequence with the field notes and tape, thus showing that the photographic record hasn't been tampered with.

Many times, I will also make a videotape of the evidence, scene, or area. A video is good, if you can get it into evidence. Remember that a video can be freeze-framed or stopped and individual screen shots can be made into pictures. By having both video and still pictures, you may get one format into evidence, even if the other is stricken by the judge.

In some cases, recording the location of the evidence can also include measuring and diagramming its location. For example, if you find a wallet dropped by a thief, it would be important to measure the distance to the broken window and show that the wallet lay in the escape route or the entry route the thief took. If you're measuring skidmarks from an auto case, the lane location, the length, the width, and location on the roadway need documentation along with your photos. This all shows the condition and circumstances under which evidence is found. In many cases, even the weather and temperature are important to the record. In shooting pictures of objects, such as a surface mark, it is a good idea to lay a 6-inch ruler in the shot or a pen so the viewer can comprehend the size and width compared to a known common object. Remember, a picture can be worth a thousand words.

To preserve the chain of possession, it's critical to document the name of the clerk, the time, the date, the photography lab, when you deliver film to be developed, and when you pick the photos up. With evidence, it's important to document where it's been at all times since it was collected.

Collect Physical Evidence

Open your kit. Use tweezers when handling evidence that might later be tested for fingerprints: a letter, a check, jewelry, a roach clip, clothing, broken glass, a drinking glass, a jewelry box, a drawer pull, lipstick tubes, prophylactic wrappers, and condoms. A professional can take fingerprints off items later that rubber gloves or clothing might obscure.

If there's a stain—on a car seat, for example—swab it with a cotton swab that's first dipped in the distilled water (the distilled water is for use on dried stains), then seal the swab in a manila envelope to send to the lab. The ideal method would be to cut the material itself and send that in, but the hole left in the seat cover of your spouse's Porsche might piss them off.

In packaging evidence, be careful what you place in plastic bags, especially organic material. For instance, damp stains, such as semen or blood, will be ruined in plastic due to bacteria growth. Damp stains should be thoroughly dried before packaging.

Keep all evidence-collection materials such as cotton swabs, cotton balls, and lift tape in sealed containers so the tools themselves are not contaminated.

Label Each Piece of Evidence

No matter what kind of evidence it is, no matter how it is collected—by a PI, a cop, or a private citizen—it should be properly labeled as the first step for it to stand up as legal evidence. The primary purpose of tagging and marking evidence is for later recall and credibility. If there is legal action, most evidence isn't used immediately. It could be a year before the evidence is presented and you want to be prepared to name the exact circumstances and date when a document or object was secured.

A small, handwritten tag that attaches with a string (for objects) and an adhesive label or scotch tape on the reverse side (for documents) will do nicely. A Post-it® is not secure enough. The ideal method is to put the evidence into a sealed container, such as a manila envelope, and label the container. In some cases, if the evidence is small, you will want to use an inner envelope as well.

Storage of Evidence

All evidence must be kept under lock and key; otherwise you cannot testify that you know for a fact that it has not been altered or tampered with. The key to the lock needs to be in your possession only. A lock box works fine for small articles, or a locked storage locker, or even a locked room that no one else has access to.

If you leave the evidence lying on the front seat of your unlocked car while shopping at Wally World, you just ruined the evidence by not maintaining security. You may have also destroyed it by letting it sit in the car in 100-degree heat for 3 hours.

Most police supply houses sell "evidence tape" as well. This is a special sealing tape you can use on a box or enclosure. If the enclosure is tampered with, the tap breaks and is not repairable. If you seal the envelope with it, you can testify that the evidence is in the same condition as when you placed it inside. You may also sign your name in ink across the flap to help insure that it has remained sealed and in the same envelope as when it was packaged.

In many cases, you'll want to turn evidence over to your lawyer to provide that extra cushion of legal guardianship for the panties, the phone bills, and the videotapes.

Testing Evidence

Before you spend your hard-earned money on a lab, there are many presumptive test kits on the market that will tell you if something is cocaine, semen, marijuana, etc. A private lab is going to charge you big bucks for the test, regardless if it is positive or not.

Substances

However, there are many private labs around the country that will conduct lab tests for private citizens: DNA, fingerprints, semen, drug use, identification of metals, substances, soil, poisons (is that arsenic in the tea?), hair, and paternity testing.

Fingerprints

You can send anything off for fingerprint testing to a private professional who is certified in fingerprint techniques and latent-print identification. If you ever wondered whatever happened to retired FBI agents, now you know. You won't have access to the database, but you can use the results to compare prints from other sources.

Remember that a fingerprint card is also public record in most states. You could save a few bucks by getting a good copy of the card and submitting it along with the prints to your expert for identification. Fingerprint cards can also be obtained from professional licensing applications, as most states require it as part of the application process.

If you know evidence has been handled by, say, you and your husband, you also need to submit your prints to the expert for elimination. You can get your prints taken at any local police station for about five bucks. People applying for a license do it all the time.

Maintain the Chain of Evidence: The Log

To be legally sound, evidence must be maintained in a "chain." The legal chain of evidence is the unbroken record of who had it at all times, where it was located, and when it was given over to another person. This is known as an evidence log. I attach this log right to the evidence for signatures when I give it to a lab, or another person, such as a lawyer. This is usually a handwritten piece of paper attached to an evidence container with tape or a staple. But evidence can be anything from a stack of money to a car. For an object like a rifle, the evidence log is attached with a piece of wire. Sometimes the log can be kept right on the envelope holding the panties, cigarette butt, paper drinking cup, T-shirt, piece of tissue, or a cotton swab with a DNA sample. Each time a piece of sealed and labeled evidence is moved, a complete notation must be made on the evidence log to preserve the chain of evidence.

I always get a receipt as well from the person I give evidence to. I keep these receipts in a separate place, in case any evidence goes missing. Although this may be out of the league of a civilian private eye, some evidence, such as organic material, must be stored in special ways so it does not become affected by bacteria growth. You may need to research this according to the type of evidence you are collecting. A good website to find such guidelines is www.crime-scene-investigator. net/collect.html.

SPYWARE: RECOMMENDED PRIVATE-EYE EQUIPMENT

DEPENDING ON YOUR mission or objective, you may or may not need any or all of the following basic equipment. As with anything, you can choose the cheaper equipment that's perfectly sufficient for a do-it-yourselfer, or you can buy the mirrored shades and go for the high-tech, cutting-edge spyware—a lot of it the size of a pack of cigarettes—used by professionals. I've included both choices in the following list. My goal is to provide you with the specs for the essential and traditional tools of the trade.

Video Camera
Low-tech
Video is preferred over a still camera because things develop quickly and you don't want to be winding and clicking your camera during the one second of ass grabbing. Although you should bring camera as a backup, one minute of videotape is the equivalent of 500

still photographs. You need to catch it all. You can always print selected still photos from the videotape.

On the cheaper side, you can buy a 8mm videocam now for less than $200, and that will work just fine for most surveillance. They have a good zoom and are a great bargain, although they will be outdated very soon.

The preferred is an 8mm because you get longer run time. This is essential spyware these days, but it doesn't have to be top of the line. A small 8mm camcorder would be the best, a VHS camcorder would be second best.

High-tech

High-tech cameras are basically all digital. I use the Sony brand videocams which include built-in "see in the dark" features called "nightshot" and "super nightshot." This allows you to film for a limited distance in total darkness. When choosing a high-end cam, look for the best optical zoom. A 10x optical zoom with a digital zoom of at least 700x is good.

The models are changing rapidly and many of the newer ones offer recording to DVD as well as to a digital chip, such as a memory stik or smart-media card. The cams are almost palm-sized now and very convenient to carry and hide. In fact, Panasonic now makes one that is the size of a microcassette recorder or about the size of a pack of cigarettes. This unit has limited zoom ability and would be good for undercover work at very close range.

Still Camera
Low-tech

If you're really on a tight budget, then even a $10 disposable might capture the one image you need. If the image is small because of distance, you can have a developer blow up the image and crop it and still get what you want.

For a backup still camera, the preferred is a 35mm with a 200mm zoom (I always have my agents bring a camera in case the video camera fails). A high-tech camera is great, but a simple, easy-to-use one will do. Yes, it will be a grainy picture, but we are not after art as much as we are identifiable images here. A number of these standard cameras can be found on the market from about $60 and up.

If you must use a film camera, be sure it is 35mm and has some form of basic zoom as well as a manual override for the flash. A 3x zoom is the most common found on general-use 35mm cameras. If possible, you want a single-lens reflex for surveillance with interchangeable lens. Use the highest speed film your camera will take because most of this work is low-light work or people in motion. The higher the speed, the more light gathering. Standard color film will go as high as a speed of 3200. Konica ASA 3200 color is a good choice. Kodak TMAX 3200 black and white is great for low light and can be push-processed by the lab to ASA 6400. There are some cases where black and white will serve better than color because black and white is more light sensitive in dark settings. Sometimes, it's the identifiable image we would rather have than color or quality. Don't forget batteries or film for the camera.

High-tech

Any camera is better than no camera, but some are better than others for this type of work. Like other technology, this field is changing daily and is moving rapidly to all digital. Many people still use the 35mm-format cameras, but it is rapidly falling to the wayside for general use.

DX CAMERAS

The DX film canister cameras are great for small size and good features. I use a Canon Elph 2 with a 3x zoom built in. This camera is limited to ASA 400 speed film; however, its small size and features make it a natural as a PI's pocket camera. The Elph is smaller than a pack of cigarettes and easily slips into a shirt pocket or the palm of your hand.

The camera has a panoramic mode, close-up or portrait mode, and a normal mode. It also has a self-timer, and an auto flash with override, all for about $150.

DIGITAL CAMERAS

The digital camera poses a problem because of time delay, but it also represents the wave of the future. The digital camera can be purchased for as little as $30, for a point-and-shoot model with quality of 2 megapixels or less. The digital you will want for this work should be no less than 3 megapixels and have a 3x zoom, a view screen, and manual flash override as a minimum.

The Nikons and Canons are well-known brands with a variety of cameras to fit most budgets. Many of the new digital cameras also feature the ability to shoot a few seconds of video as an added feature. Digital is a nice format, as the pictures can be sent via e-mail to your lawyer in short order. They can also be cropped and enlarged on your PC to create that certain "Kodak moment" that's going to roast your opponent's butt in hell.

UNDERCOVER CAMERAS

For undercover work or for use in very close range with normal daylight, you can get a digital camera that's the size and shape of a credit card. This camera is available at Radio Shack for about $60. Place it inside an empty cigarette pack with a small hole for the photo button and you're an instant James Bond. Recently, a digital spy camera housed in a cigarette lighter has become available for about $50 on eBay. Some great buys can be found there using the search term "spy camera." These are all fixed-focus, fixed-lens, point-and-shoot cameras.

Casio, the watchmaker, sells a nifty wristwatch for about $150 that will take up to eighty photos. The watch can be downloaded to your PC using its wireless infrared feature. The watch is set up so that when you shoot a picture, it looks like you're merely checking your watch.

At www.supercircuits.com, you can find a unique motion-sensor camera that is self-contained and about the size of a pack of cigarettes. This motion-sensor camera has a media card in it and is capable of shooting 3,000 frames of video when motion is detected in an area. This unit sells for about $390 and has a fixed-focus lens. Just insert the batteries, sit it down, and check it later for that special shot.

Binoculars

Low-tech

A $19 pair of cheap binoculars that can fold up and be hidden in your pocket are sufficient, but a set of binoculars is essential. The best type of binoculars to use in this case would be something small and convenient with at least an 8x magnification—small enough to be easily concealed in a jacket pocket should someone approach your vehicle.

I try to use a smaller set with a 7x power or higher. Tasco makes an inexpensive model that folds up for your pocket and sells for about $25 at most department stores. These are adequate for city-streets work in residential or business areas.

High-tech

If your work will be in more open spaces, you will need to move up to a 10x power. One model I use is made by Simmons and features a 15x zoom lever and is still a pocket-sized unit. You hear me mention pocket-sized a lot because if you need to get out on foot, you certainly will be noticed if you look like Rambo with all kinds of gear hanging from you. Better to wear a vest with several roomy pockets and have a hidden arsenal of high-tech devices unseen by passersby.

THE BINO-CAMERA COMBO

Meade makes a set of binoculars that also contains a digital camera that takes about thirty good still pictures of what you are looking at through them. Very simple to operate, it's sold by such stores as Radio Shack and others. The best part is that they can be bought new for about $50. Simply download the pictures via a USB slot on your PC and have them on your attorney's desk by morning!

Audiotape Recorder
Low-tech

Almost any microcassette will do for recording your evidence log, keeping surveillance notes, and taping a witness. This can be obtained for as little as $25 at most major department stores. This will become handy because, as you conduct your surveillance, describe a scene, and discover evidence, you will want to make as many notes as possible. You'll want to document dates evidence was collected or a mark entered a building. You'll also need to make sure that during your surveillance you have a notepad and a pen.

A word of caution here: There are many laws regulating who and how you can record. Check federal and local and state laws in your area, as they change rapidly. Under certain circumstances, you may record telephone conversations, but it's changing so fast, you need to check the law on this first. Don't get cute and make an illegal taped conversation and end up facing a criminal charge.

High-tech

A VOX (voice activation) feature is nice, too, but not mandatory. And it's best if the recorder you select has a microphone jack, an earphone jack, and if possible, a remote jack.

THE ART OF DUMPSTER DIVING

GOING THROUGH A subject's garbage on a regular basis is the method by which I have solved the majority of my cases, and the law is on your side to use this highly effective form of information and evidence collection. As long as the trash is on the curb, it's been deemed in court cases to be legal for anyone to take. The assumption is that it's unwanted property. The IRS and FBI use it all the time.

However, if the trash is next to the house, your taking the trash out is actually stealing. It's illegal. You need to wait until your mark moves it to the curb before you can get your grubby hands on it. Hopefully, wearing latex gloves.

You also need to do this undetected so you can pull the trash over a period of time. Thus, like most private investigation, you need to prepare, case the location, and wait.

Case the Scene

Does the subject set the trash out at night or morning? What color and type of garbage bags does the target use? Stuff the same type of garbage bags with newspapers. What is the time of the pickup? Conduct surveillance, ask neighbors, or call public utilities to get the time.

Prepare and Execute

- Arrive a half hour before pickup. If pickup is at 10:00, arrive at 9:30.

- Pull up in front, next to the curb.

- Grab bags from the can and replace them with your dummy bags.

You're done in thirty seconds. Anyone who sees the garbage won't notice any differently because the bags look the same, even to the garbage men. You leave undetected, which is key if you have intentions of doing this more than once.

Time to Dive

- Go to a remote location.

- Select a place where you won't be bothered by wind.

- Be sure you're in a well-ventilated area when opening bags.

- Empty the bags and spread them out.

- Put on rubber gloves and start sorting.

- Document your finds (with a tape recorder, camcorder, or paper and pen).

- Package and label evidence important to the case.

- Save envelopes. Return addresses and names of businesses are important.

What You're Looking For

- Financial statements (credit card, bank, stock, trust, corporation, and business accounts with, if you're lucky, the account number, location, and amount)

- Envelopes from financial institutions with return addresses

- Any torn paper, especially if deliberately torn into pieces. Try to match the pieces and put into one bag to reconstruct later

- Love letters, cards, and other incriminating correspondence

What You'll Find

A person's entire life is in their garbage. You'll know what the target had to drink, what the target ate for dinner, and which bill collectors are after him or her. Prescription bottles may indicate medical problems you didn't know of. You may find a note indicating the subject is getting ready to move. In one case, I found a person had a corporation in Panama to which he had shifted funds. Eventually, the FBI got in on that case. The evidence was the envelope from a bank in Panama. The bank name led to the actual account in Panama.

Most people are creatures of habit. The garbage helps you determine a target's habits, things that could be important for surveillance. In these bags will be the detritus of a lifestyle: food packages, dog-track tickets, empty bath products, evidence of a pet (important for surveillance), the target's brand of cigarette. You'll get a clear sense of the mark's lifestyle. Does he or she drink espresso or plain coffee? Look at the grocery receipts. Are there notes and phone numbers of friends and relatives? I've even found a mark scribbled notes on her plotting to leave with the kids.

You'll also find out other things which might be important to an intelligence file if not assets recovery: stems and seeds from marijuana separation and other evidence of drugs; lewd magazines; Polaroids of people in compromising positions; and, as my operatives found out, in the worse case scenario, soiled diapers. My guys had to drive back with their heads hanging out of the window. All are clues that have solved cases.

INDEX